Have Tarot Will Party:

A Comprehensive Guide to Party Reading for the Tarot Professional

By Jenna Matlin

Copyright 2019 © Jenna Matlin

All rights reserved. No part of this book may be reproduced in any form or by any electronic or mechanical means, including information storage and retrieval systems, without written permission from the author, except in the case of a reviewer, who may quote brief passages embodied in critical articles or in a review.

Trademarked names appear throughout this book. Rather than use a trademark symbol with every occurrence of a trademarked name, names are used in an editorial fashion, with no intention of infringement of the respective owner's trademark.

The information in this book is distributed on an "as is" basis, without warranty. Although every precaution has been taken in the preparation of this work, neither the author nor the publisher shall have any liability to any person or entity with respect to any loss or damage caused or alleged to be caused directly or indirectly by the information contained in this book.

Photo used with permission by Julia Haines

Contents

Reader's Invocation
Preface
Foreword
Introduction

Chapter 1: Gotta Start Somewhere
Readers Are Made, Not Born
Origin Story
Merrymaking Oracles
Get Paid
Rule Minders
Rookie Problems
Get Booked
Money>Exposure
Charitable Acts

Chapter 2: Training the Host
Preparation is 90% of Your Work
Map It
Set-up
Guest Count

Right Price
Between Time
Format & Flow

Chapter 3: Dancing in the Dark
Make Friends with Ambiguity and Uncertainty
House Parties
Non-Hosted Events
Hired Help
Freebie Fifteen
Rotten Hosts
Happy Hour
Public Events
Spatial Needs
Buddy System
Corporate Events
Tip Me
Event Companies
Devilish Details

Chapter: 4 It's Go Time
When the Deck Hits the Table
Massive Bandwidth
Self-Care
Repetitive Motion
Liquid Effects

Line Management
Your Table
Fashion Plate
Auditory Warning
Draw the Line
Safety First
Drinking & Reading
Bad Actors
Mandatory Choices
Do the Shuffle
Reading Choreography
Quick or Thorough
Reading Sequence
Tarot Don't Care
Gallery Readings
At Ease, Reader
Party Guests
Travel Kit
Repeat Business

Chapter: 5 Vibe Attracts Tribe

What's Your Frequency, Reader?
Metaphysical Properties
Grounding and Centering
Protect Yourself
Clear the Air

Conclusion
Closing Blessing

Appendices
Sample Proposal Letter
Sample Contract
Sample Host Letter
Sample Receipt
General Disclaimer for Tarot Services
Party Pack List
General Party Reading Spread

After Party
Acknowledgments
About the Author

Reader's Invocation

May the source of all that is Good, all that is Worthy, and all that is Meaningful speak to me through the cards.

May I be a kind interpreter, a helpful guide, and a noble facilitator of the story.

May I use my privileged position to increase perception, to foster compassion, and to perceive Spirit.

May I cast the lamp of insight high enough for clear vision: high enough to chase away the shadows of doubt, fear, and resistance.

May I withhold whatever is not helpful, what is unkind, and what is not ready.

May the weary feel the comfort of my care, the warmth of my affection, and the strength of my objective desire to witness their unfolding.

May I use tarot to guide and not to punish, to recommend and not to condemn.

May I be a servant to the Soul.

May I be a servant to the Message.

Most of all, may all who come feel safe.

Preface

In the past, I've made proposals to write a fully comprehensive tarot business book to several well-known publishers. I was turned down because this—a niche within a niche subject—would not generate enough money to make it worth their time. They have a point; I'm writing to a small section of the population. You and I are certainly not mainstream.

Every writer knows that writing a book is a labor of love. I will not be compensated for the sheer time I've spent to write it. So why do I write a little how-to book for such a specific population of people?

I wrote this slim volume because I'm deeply passionate about tarot as a professional practice. My hope is that we who love to read will continue to professionalize the work of tarot. By tarot becoming accepted as a modality that has merit, we will be able to gain respectability, throw off the pseudonyms we claimed out of fear, and tell strangers and friends alike that yes, we are tarot readers, and we are damn proud of the work we do.

When people are exposed to high-quality tarot experiences, they are forced to question their own knee-jerk assumptions. When we are able to practice without fear, we are able to dismantle the stigma and bias many of us face. **This book and its how-to methods are, in a small way, my part in crafting this greater cultural shift.**

The other reason why I wrote this book is that the vast majority of readers are not naturally good at business. We are healers, first. We don't know how to sell ourselves, and we don't want to bother people. We often assume that business people are smarmy capitalists who care more about money than others. I certainly had that thought until I became a business owner myself. I discovered that having my own business meant that I could help people without any ethical dilemmas.

In fact, my business is the most honest and heartfelt work I've ever done. No politics, no fuzzy grey corporate lines, no office tyrants, no white lies. In fact, there are none of the things I remember having to do just to survive in a typical office environment. By having this business, I'm able to do more of what I love: helping others. I can also say no to anything that feels out of alignment with who and what I am. These noes allow me to say many more yesses.

It was with this revolutionary shift in my attitude towards business that I was able to become successful. It saddens me when an excellent reader hides away because the work of business ownership is daunting. When a reader operates under the assumption (like I did) that asking for money is dirty work, it can stop us from doing the thing we are meant to do. *It's through creating a business that we can do more of the work we love.*

The world needs your spark now more than ever. People are looking for a source of clarity, wisdom, and truth. If I can, in some small way, help you embrace the business aspects in addition to the tarot reading part, then together we can bring this beautiful craft to more people. You will be sustained by creating strong practices that support you.

Foreword

My very first professional tarot gig was a psychic fair back in 1994 or so. There, fellow readers shared some business advice with me. They all agreed I should make cultivating tarot party business a priority. One reader, consulting her own cards, nodded sagely and said, "Oh, yes, you will do very well with parties." Quickly she gave me a five-minute crash course based on her party reading experiences. That was the whole of my training to become a party tarot reader. Then ensued a few months that could have made me doubt that prediction.

My first party clients often didn't have a table for me to use. After one evening of sitting on the end of a waterbed and using an ironing board for a tarot table, I learned to carry a small folding table and chair in my car trunk. This was before cellphones, GPS and online mapping services. I discovered that clients often didn't know the name of their street, their closest highway exit or even their left from their right. Finding my way to some of those parties was evidence of my psychic ability, as many directions began with "Do you know where the old tree used to be?" That none of these frustrations discouraged me from pursuing party business was a testament to the potential that I saw in gathering people to experience tarot reading together.

Eventually parties became fun and profitable, and I learned something important. Good parties beget better parties, and all parties beget new clients. Parties also provide an opportunity for folks who wouldn't normally seek out a reading to experience what an unexpectedly helpful, healing and entertaining thing a tarot reading can be.

I can imagine that, if I had access to a book like this one back in the mid-1990s, my entry into the world of tarot parties and corporate gigs might have been a little smoother. Jenna's candid stories of some of her early mishaps will be comforting to experienced readers and enlightening to newer ones.

Those who have read Jenna's first book, *Have Tarot Will Travel*, know that one of her superpowers is to quantify things that feel amorphous and create actionable steps to do things that would otherwise seem uncertain. She's done that in this book as well, creating logical systems and protocols to help you create your successful tarot party business, and avoid some mishaps along the way.

Christiana Gaudet
January 2018
Palm City, FL

Introduction

Have Tarot Will Party is a down-to-earth how-to guide for the tarot reading professional. This book was born from my years of experience as a tarot party professional, and it includes my best practices as well as my mistakes. This book is the culmination of three conference workshops as well as a tarot summer school offering. This means that I was able to create a focus group on the topic to determine what tarot practitioners needed most. I listened deeply to the questions that participants asked and wrote this book emphasizing aspects most puzzling to my students.

I've also tried to keep some elements similar to my first book, *Have Tarot Will Travel*. Consider this book to be a companion piece to the first. If you have not gotten that book, then I recommend you do so because festival readings are different to party readings, especially in the behind-the-scenes aspects.

I wrote *Have Tarot Will Party* sequentially. I take you through things as they become relevant from the beginning stages of building a party reading practice, to negotiating with hosts, to guiding you through the actual party, and finally the follow-up once you are done. I also include a comprehensive appendix chock-full of sample documents you are free to use as inspiration for the ones you'll eventually create for your business.

In short, I tried to share everything I could from my experiences so that I can prepare you for what you'll face. I tell many stories about what I learned, but the names are changed to protect the individuals.

Finally, this book is not the sole authority. My way is not the only way of doing party readings. I'm sure there are other techniques and procedures that work just as well if not better. Please see this as a guide for inspiration. Take what works and leave the rest.

1
Gotta Start Somewhere
Readers Are Made, Not Born

Origin Story

My first professional reading experience was at a party. In fact, it was because of party readings that I eventually decided to become a full-time professional. It all began at the tender age of fourteen. I was gifted with my first tarot deck by a neighbor who had become an unofficial uncle of mine. In my neighborhood there were several households of vibrant, fun, and funny men who were active in the local drag queen scene. Often, I would stop by to watch one sewing up a new outfit or just hang out drinking "virgin" options of whatever they were having. These guys had an immense and positive impact on my life—an impact that I could only fully appreciate much later.

A few months after giving me my first deck, they invited me to read tarot for their "Victor/Victoria" party for Halloween. I charged five dollars for each reading and was busy the whole night. I was astounded by tarot's ability to get right to the heart of the matter. I was shocked to see how our age differences melted away under the truth and vigor of tarot. I remember a young man telling me how much I helped him that night. I was hooked.

Over the next twenty years or so, I would read at parties hosted by friends and other close connections. At parties I usually can be found in the corner petting the resident cat, but as a tarot reader, I have a job. My intermittent social anxiety melted away once I knew I had a role that connected with people.

Fast forward to my current business where party readings are a nice segment of my work. Even though I currently have enough one-to-one clients to support my business, I also like to read at parties to switch things up. For a small business such as mine, the more income streams I have, the more stable my revenue is. I had to learn the hard way, however, to be successful as a reader for parties.

Party readings are different from private sessions. I get to crack jokes, tease a little, and maybe even flirt if I feel like it. Perhaps it's the Gemini in me, but I love the juxtaposition of light heartedness and serious wisdom. Where else can I tell guests, "The more you drink the more accurate I become"? Through laughter, we are able to reach people who would be otherwise closed off. As they say, laughter is the best medicine.

Of course, tarot parties can be daunting. Putting our skills out to all who come is an incredibly vulnerable act. We are exposing ourselves to naysayers, skeptics and ne'er-do-wells. But let me just say this, especially for those of you who only work online for these very fears: *people are far, far kinder in person than they are online*. When people cannot hide behind a screen, it's incredible how mindful they can become. When we meet face-to-face, we are more apt to see the humanity in one another. From there you have an opportunity to cause a shift in their world view.

Pretty heady stuff.

Merrymaking Oracles

Reading tarot at party venues can be rewarding, challenging, and everything in between. Adding party readings to your repertoire requires a list of skills and a particular knowledge base that is distinct from festival or one-to-one readings. Gigs on the weekend or evenings can support your day job or help you transition from a part-time reader into a full-time one. Reading at parties is a great way to have people sample your style in a non-threatening environment. If you do a good job, the bookings will easily flow because you'll get referrals from the guests.

Party readings will put you into contact with all kinds of people. Bachelorette parties, high-end corporate events, store openings, intimate holiday get-togethers, parties on boats, in mansions and among gardens are just some of the parties you may read tarot for. It's simply impossible to become bored as a reader for party venues.

Like festival readings, you are typically seeing people back-to-back and in quick succession. However, you are reading for people who are usually not paying. You are seen more as an entertainer than an oracle. You'll be reading to the bored, the uninitiated, the curious, the drunk, and the skeptical. This can be daunting for sure. *Here, you are not reading to the converted. You'll be doing the converting!*

Being a party reader does require a certain type of individual. This person is usually outgoing, (or, like me, an introvert who plays a convincing extrovert) flexible, a careful planner, and above all, a professional. Often you are an employee of the host, and as such you'll need to be able to take direction. The expectations of party readings can be intense, but the monetary reward is commensurate to those demands. Some readers work exclusively for parties and make a living doing just that.

You'll need to quickly sense who is sitting at your table and how to best read for them. Within seconds, you'll have to decide how to deliver information, what questions you'll answer, and do it in a way your host finds acceptable. It doesn't mean that you don't take the cards seriously, but your delivery needs to enhance the party atmosphere. No needle-scratching-the-record predictions, folks! Now, some readers don't want to be considered entertainment—fair enough and for good reason. But if you have a sense of humor about it, then this can certainly work for you.

Get Paid

You deserve to be paid. You deserve a livable wage for your work. There is a troubling drumbeat in the spiritual community. Namely, it goes to the tune of "You are doing spiritual work; therefore, you should not be paid for it." Some readers internalize that erroneous message and feel shame when asking for remuneration.

Let's look at this more deeply: I have a good friend who is an Episcopal priest. In fact, I took him with me when I predicted the Super Bowl on the radio. I think the DJ kind of freaked out that I brought a priest with me (he was even in his collar!)–but that is a story for another time. Anyway, my friend works so hard to care for his parish, and guess what? This dude gets paid. The Imam down the street? Yeah, he has a salary. The Rabbi that lives nearby is paid by his community so he can serve it. The same goes for shamans, root workers, and just about everyone. In what world do any religious or spiritual workers only eat air and sunshine? They don't. Even nuns who take a vow of poverty are provided with lodging, clothes, a monthly stipend, and health insurance.

Clients will absolutely pick up any hedging you have about money. They will sense the hesitation in your voice, and since everyone is looking for a deal, they will pay you what you ask for–not necessarily what you deserve. If you have any lingering resistance to expecting money for your work, it will affect your business. The emotions you secretly feel are actually energy that you are broadcasting on everything.

Speak with confidence, demand your worth, and your clients will see the worth in you. You are no less "spiritual" because of it. Your gifts were given to you to use and to make a living with! This is true for every living system in our planet. The apple tree doesn't make fruit just for the hell of it. It buries seeds deep inside so they will be carried away and planted. Everything here is an exchange. When you speak your worth, you are right in alignment with all things.

Rule Minders

The tarot community is filled with strange rules. *Never let anyone touch your deck. Your first deck must be gifted to you. Never drink while reading.* There seems to be a litany of old wives' tales that can limit what someone does and how they do it—for no real reason at all besides personal belief. If you are a part of online tarot communities, you have surely encountered the shrewish cries of people telling you what you can't or mustn't or shouldn't ever do with your tarot deck. I find these limiting more than helpful.

I am especially troubled by the way that some people in the tarot community look down on party readings. There are some professional readers out there who think that party readings are not as spiritual or as deep as one-to-one work. I am here to tell you that, as someone who does both and as someone who does one-to-one client work as the bulk of my practice, they are dead wrong.

In fact, there is a beautiful kind of mysticism that happens when you are an entertainment reader. You are able to dispense quick and hearty readings to people who need it the most. You are in the trenches, giving advice, dispensing hope, and crafting meaning in the hard spaces. Sure, you are seen as "entertainment," but entertainment can be life changing. Have we not been totally changed as people after watching a movie or reading a book? I argue that, through the very aegis of entertainment, you can craft incredible wonder and indelible insight. Don't ever let anyone think less of you for doing this work—*least of all yourself.* What you do is vitally important.

Tarot is amazing, tarot is mystical, tarot is incredible, and tarot is robust—especially that last part. Tarot has existed for hundreds of years because it's durable and user-friendly. Trust that it will deliver the message. Feel free to give certain techniques a try but lay them aside if they do not add to your practice. Question the rules you hear. Most importantly, though, trust yourself to create a system that works for you—even if no one else understands why you must jump three times while rubbing your belly and patting your head before each reading on a Tuesday. Your relationship to tarot is yours alone, and that is sacred. Allow tarot's beautiful egalitarianism work with you and let the rest fall away.

Rookie Problems

I certainly made some fool-hardy mistakes when adding party readings to my repertoire. Unfortunately, in the land of the internet, those unhappy guests (and their reviews of me) will live forever in infamy. They are a constant reminder of my failure. As with most things, however, it's in our darkest moments that we learn the most.

When I was just beginning to build my client base, I turned to a large "discount coupon" company. This company sent out drastically reduced coupons to their email base. After their cut, I was making very little. But the exposure to my local area was irresistible to me and ultimately worth it. I was thrilled to see so many people visiting my website after my deal went live. At the time I didn't have an office, so I was seeing clients in my home or travelling to their location. A few groups would buy the deal individually then pool them together as an extremely cheap entertainment option for their parties. I cringe looking back at how badly I was taken advantage of. I was so desperate to launch my business that had really bad boundaries which attracted the wrong kind of people.

One such group of women asked me to come to their home for a tarot party. There were about six women who bought the deal. I was given the apartment address, and on a chilly, stormy night I headed out to the host's place. It was a thirty-minute drive to an unfamiliar part of town. When I got there, I was astounded to find that it was a huge building complex. The address took me to the first building, but I could not see that there were other apartments behind the first, and the front door required me to be buzzed in. The hostess gave me none of these details, and I didn't think to ask.

I was locked out of the building. I called my host several times, but it just rang and rang. This was right before smartphones, and all I had was a flip phone. I was unable to look up information online, nor could I email her.

I wandered around the apartment complex for forty-five minutes, and almost no one came and went. It was dark and cold. I felt unsafe walking in the large parking lot at night with my laptop. I called my friend at the time and said, "I don't know what to do. I guess I'm going to leave. I know I'm going to pay for this." I felt a lump of dread in my throat as I drove away, but I honestly didn't know what else to do.

Right before getting home, the hostess finally called me, a full forty-five minutes after the time I was supposed to start. Totally apologetic, I explained what happened. She stated that she sent everyone a detailed email about getting into her apartment, but I never got that email. She demanded that I turn around and drive back to the party. By then I was frazzled, upset, and had already spent two hours commuting and searching for her party.

I told her that I had another gig lined up later that night and could not return (since I was only using those deals, I had to book many in order to make a profit). I was prepared to schedule another time with her. At that point, she called me a liar and said that I "Ditched them to go to a better gig." I told her that I took issue with being called a liar and that I would not return. I advised her to get a refund from the deal company. I cannot and will not read for anyone who insults my integrity or dignity.

The next couple of days were serious drama. Both the host and her friends made up outrageous lies about my non-appearance to the deal company (that I had to fix). They also left horrible reviews about me online. The host and her friends harassed and threatened me via email. It was an extremely painful and hard lesson, but it taught me a lot.

I was at fault as much as the host was. I didn't triple check the location. I didn't follow up with the host. I didn't have a contract. I didn't have a contingency plan in place. So, I got a Smartphone. I also learned to speak with the host day-of and specifically ask for logistics about the event location, parking, and whether there is anything else I need to know. I double check phone numbers and text the host when I'm on my way, requesting a response. Most importantly, I learned that if I didn't value my services then my guests wouldn't either, so I raised my prices accordingly.

I learned to document the heck out of every interaction and to be detail-oriented about the whole process. Honestly, details are not my thing. I do not naturally go from A to B in an orderly fashion, so I had to train myself to follow a procedure. Once I did this, everything became smoother.

As psychologically traumatizing as my first experiences in professional party readings were for me, I'm glad that I didn't let that stop me. As you begin doing tarot parties, you'll absolutely make mistakes. Some of those mistakes might be painful. I encourage you to see them for the learning lessons they are so that they can propel you to greater performance rather than seeming like a "sign" that you shouldn't do them.

Get Booked

When you are ready to add party readings to your repertoire, you can begin by hosting your own party or by having a close friend or family member host one for you. Make it free for everyone. Consider these practice rounds as a beta test for your whole flow. While it's free (there are only a couple of situations where I recommend giving free readings), you might want to tell the guests that the reading is in exchange for honest feedback and give them a form to fill out anonymously. Have them do it before they leave, otherwise you will likely never get them back. Your beta test party should have elements in it that will be true to when you go pro such as the back-to-back element and timed readings for each guest. I recommend doing two or three of these parties before going pro if you can.

Record your sessions. Yes, listen to yourself! I know it's hard to listen to yourself, but this is the best way for you to critique yourself on your delivery, your listening skills, your style, and your pacing.

After you have done a few test runs and are feeling ready to go live, ask your friends and relatives to host you for a party. First, you want to leverage the people you already know and focus on home-based parties. When I first started, I did the Tupperware method of booking parties. Each host got a free thirty-minute session with me outside of the party as a "thank you" incentive. Also, each guest pays their own way. Your goal is to get at least one booking for another party from the guests you are reading for. I recommend doing this for about six months. House parties will have more of the "already converted" type of guests, and since you are most likely connected through a friend or family member, they will be easier to read for and more forgiving on timing and style. These are the people you want to hone your craft with. You need to build your confidence. This is a priority, so it's important not to push yourself so far out of your comfort zone that you swear off party readings. You want to build your skill and confidence level step-by-step.

Once you have nailed your craft with friends and family, it is time to read for strange people. Yes, strangers! This one of few exceptions I make regarding working for free. Since you are just starting out, now is a great time to reach out to your local nonprofit community. These guys are always throwing fundraisers and would be delighted to have a tarot reader for free. You can run them through all of your contract details and reading format. If there are kinks, you are volunteering so they can't really complain too much. You can also have your promotional items out for the party goers to book you at a later date.

Then the next step is to reach out to local businesses. For example, hit up all the hair salons within a ten-mile radius to offer your services. Small businesses routinely have customer appreciation days or holiday specials. Your presence is a draw and will bring more people to their event. Make some postcards about tarot parties to hand out to your potential hosts. Offer to come in and do a free lunch time tarot hour with all the stylists (another rare time that I recommend doing readings for free) so they can sample your wares.

As a rule, target women-focused and women-owned businesses. I say this because, in general, these businesses will be more open about having a tarot reader at their place of work. Go in and talk to the owners. Give them your card. Pound the pavement like the good old days. This works. Trust me on this one. Your goal at this point is to start building your party guest base. Yes, this is scary. Yes, they can say no. Yes, sometimes they will scrunch up their face like you're a big turd. Ignore the haters. Keep knocking until the doors open, and they will open.

While you are doing in-person introductions, you also want an online presence. There are websites just for entertainers for parties. These sites allow you to post a profile, and you can bid on gigs through their platform. You can also place yourself on wedding or bachelorette party registries and bridal events. Do you feel comfortable reading for kids? Get connected with communities that might hire you for Bar/Bat Mitzvahs and Sweet Sixteen parties. Reach out to prom planning groups for the end of the school year. Contact local restaurants and bars. Nonprofit fundraising galas, women-centered networking and community groups are just a few examples. Parties are happening everywhere, all the time.

Contact party companies, party planners, party catering companies, and party rental companies. These usually tend towards higher-end venue events and may help you find corporate gigs. Put together a small PR folder which includes a nice letter of your intent, a postcard for tarot parties and your business card. It's totally appropriate to be creative with this.

In terms of creativity and reaching out–the sky is the limit! I've reached out to a paint-and-sip company doing paint nights for adults. The owner and I got to talking, and I became an "add on" service for other groups who wanted to do a paint night and also have a tarot reader on hand. *You see, when you remain open to possibility, possibility finds you in the most uncommon places!*

Yes, you need a website. It's easy enough to make your own website and there really is no excuse not to have one. You can even create a free one. A simple one will do. On your website, have pictures of yourself reading at parties. People want to see you in action. This is where starting out with family- or friend-based gigs can be helpful; they can take pictures of you while you are reading.

Also, grab some quotes from the feedback forms you handed out at your beginning parties and add them to your website. People want to read reviews about your work. Finally, always have a reference on hand. Ask a previous host if they would be willing to be a reference. Do some research into Search Engine Optimization (SEO) so people can find your site — or hire someone to do this for you. You want people in your area to be able to find you online. Between all of your in-person work, and your online work, you should be pretty busy.

If things start slow, don't panic. It takes time to build a reputable company and a client base. People need time to get to know you. Word of mouth can be strange as people you read for five years ago finally sends a friend your way. People will promise up and down to review you, then won't. People are busy and make promises they won't keep. Wait for no man and keep putting yourself out there. You will build trust as you get reviews and as you become known in community circles.

Word of mouth networking tends to follow lines of socioeconomic, cultural, or work groups. For example, I read for a community of Irish women in the Philadelphia area, a well-heeled 40-something community near me, as well as a community of female doctors in NYC, and another friend group in Seattle. Some clients will be super referrals and will be responsible for huge leaps in your client base while others who love you to death won't breathe a word about you to anyone else. Humans are funny and often unreliable which means you need to diversify your efforts as much as possible.

Once a tipping point hits, you will feel it. There will be a moment where all that hard work in marketing yourself will pay off. I am talking about timelines in the magnitude of years. They say it takes two-to-five years to build a viable client base. From my own experience, I agree. Tarot party readings are lucrative, but don't expect them to happen instantly.

Money>Exposure

As noted above, there are only a few occasions that I recommend working for free, and only when you are absolutely starting out. Even when you are working for free, it's because you are getting something out of it like practice or ironing out a technique. However, the sad fact of our industry is that people seem to think we don't care about being paid. Chalk this up to being an artist!

Here is an actual email I was sent by a small business owner in my area (names were changed to protect anonymity). I didn't know this person. This was a totally cold email.

Hello Jenna:

My name is Melissa Boyd

I have a small boutique on Raleigh Avenue, Melissa Boyd Boutique. On June 7th I'm hosting a girl's night out. I would be able to take appointments so it does not waste your time. My invitation is already out but I can email a message for it.

My shop is a women's accessories and jewelry boutique. I have a large backyard where I'm putting up a tent. I would have a space for you to do a private reading. I have a larger dressing room where you could probably put a small table to do your Tarot. If this is something that we could discuss, please call me at the shop tomorrow after 11:30.
I would be interested in you offering mini readings at a charge. You can then, of course, give out your card and possibly book for longer sessions at another time at your place.

What Melissa is offering is a fantastically bad deal for me. *Melissa is basically assuming that I'm okay with taking all the risk for the event.* Melissa wants the benefit of hiring an entertainer to her girl's night out, but she doesn't want to pay for it. Whether I sit there all night busy or no one comes it's all on me. Melissa has no "skin the game." If people show up because I'm there, it's even better for her, but if no one wants readings, what does it cost her?

Melissa has a small boutique, so the "gift" of exposure is minimal. Melissa also states that her mass newsletter announcing the event already went out, so there wasn't much time or effort put into promoting me. I'm tacked on at the end which is even worse. In so many ways this is a fundamentally bad offer. If I was just starting out, I might ask that she pay a base hourly rate to have me (maybe fifty percent of my regular rate) hoping that the guests will pay the rest.

Let me be clear: I've done many things for exposure. I've been interviewed on the radio and done big name events all in the name of exposure, but please learn from my mistakes. Exposure events are not worth it. I've rarely recouped the cost of attending in the first place.

If another business wants to have you as entertainment, they need to hire you! You deserve the same professional respect as a DJ or a party planner. Working for exposure is beneath you as a professional. Follow my guidelines here, and you won't feel the need to do it beyond your beginning steps.

Charitable Acts

It is always good business to occasionally give it away. Plan on deciding a certain amount of *pro bono* work per year you would like to do. About once or twice a year I give my services, *pro bono*, to nonprofits and also directly to clients in need. The great news about these (besides feeling your heart swell with compassion) is that you should be able to write off the cost of doing these events as a charitable contribution come tax time, depending on your location and relevant tax laws.

2
Training the Host
Preparation is 90% of Your Work

Most hosts don't know what to expect when hiring a tarot reader. They imagine having a reader in the corner of their event, but beyond that, they don't know how to plan for you. This is where you'll walk them through the process. You need to maintain control of your procedures at all times—both for your comfort as well as the comfort of your host and their guests. Half the conversations you'll have with the hosts will be logistical in nature. The other half will be concerning payment.

Map It

The location of the event is a factor to consider when deciding whether to accept the gig and how much to charge. I've made the mistake of quoting a price before mapping out the location and drove around for free for hours. Now, I never give a quote without first knowing where the event is located. How far away is it? Will traffic be a factor at the time and day of the event? What about parking? Driving ten miles at one in the afternoon on a Tuesday could be an hour less than driving the same route at rush hour on a Friday. In some areas, parking will be an issue and paying for parking can be expensive. Or, maybe the location is a long walk from where you can park, so you decide to take public transportation.

If you take public transportation, how long will that take you? Will the bus get you home late at night, and are there different prices depending on when you take it? If public transportation stops running, can you hail a taxi, be picked up by a friend or use a ride sharing service? All of these things need to be factored in. The last thing you want to do is arrive to the event flustered, stressed, or anxious. By doing this work ahead of time you'll arrive cool, calm, and clairvoyant.

Give yourself extra time, sometimes more than you think is necessary, especially when going to a new venue. Hosts may not remember to tell you the finer details of the venue such as where to park, how to enter the building, where the entrance is, or how to find the hostess. These are all things that can take time and should be part of the quote when you make it.

Make sure you have the phone number of the host or the event location manager (for public events) in case you get lost, are stuck in traffic, or something unforeseen happens. I recommend texting the host when you are on your way, and then text them again once you've arrived. Perhaps this is overkill, but I never want a host to wonder where I am at any point in the process. They usually have so much going on, I want worrying about me to be the least of their problems.

I get anxious when driving at night, or in a new location. I do not want to show up frazzled or stressed because I know that those things hurt my ability to read. I will take more time, unpaid, to ensure that I'm showing up calm and ready to go.

Set-up

Included in my contract is a fifteen-minute set-up time and is part of the quote I make them. In the past, I've worked with hosts, had them sign the contract, and then had them ask if I could show up thirty to forty-five minutes prior to my reading time. Essentially, they are asking if I will work that extra set-up time for free. It's important to impress on your hosts that *you are being paid for your time in total, not just the active times you might be reading.* Clearly indicate to your host that you need x amount of time to set-up before you begin reading and have that in your contract. If they want you to show up earlier than the included fifteen minutes, then they need to pay for it. Sometimes they don't understand that it takes only a few moments to bust out your deck and business cards. Some gigs will want you there during the dinner portion (even though you are not reading during the toasts) and that is fine, but remember you are being paid for your presence, not just your active reading time.

Guest Count

During the negotiation stages, I'm clear about the number of people that I can read for in an hour. I give hosts a base rate of five to eight guests an hour. During that time, I'm able to answer one question or give a mini general overview in five to ten minutes. My ballpark estimate is that we should be able to accommodate about thirty to fifty percent of the guest list as a minimum. Not every guest will want a reading, but if we go below the thirty to fifty percent mark depending, it will cause more disgruntlement than entertainment. If, for example, a host has fifty people coming, she can reasonably conclude that fifteen to twenty-five of them will want a reading. If I can read anywhere between eight to ten people an hour, the host should hire me for three and half hours, rounding up.

Sometimes it is difficult to give a firm number because the rate you quoted for x number of people is assuming that guests are instantly lining up to your table from the moment you sit down until the event is over. This is rarely the case in larger gatherings. Sometimes it might take a full thirty minutes before anyone is at your table.

People need to warm up to the idea of getting a reading. They might also be catching up with friends before they feel the need to come over to have their fortune told. Even when you have a list of the guests, they may not see the need to hurry over when their turn comes up. Even if they know it's their turn, they will say something like, "Yeah, give me one minute I'm fixing a drink or finishing up a conversation." These minutes add up! Make it clear with your host (if they have a hard number of people you are to read for) that it's up to them to get the guests to you at the appointed time. *Once again, you are not responsible for reading beyond the quoted time for free because people are tardy!*

I do not consider it my responsibility to rush people out of my chair, though I do keep my readings focused and succinct. Some hosts will want you to read faster in order to push more people into the time you were hired for, but you are not Zoltar. You are a human being, and this is an imprecise art.

For smaller parties, I recommend to the host that we need a list of people so you can get started right away. No matter what happens, it's still important for you to hold to your timeline. If guests didn't come until later, or if there is a rush at the end, keep in mind that your time is sacred. *Don't work for free.* Working for free won't give you more clients, nor will it book you more gigs. People who knowingly take advantage when you are off the clock are clients who find it okay to exploit you. Being a pushover will not pay the bills, my friend!

For large events guests may try to get you to stay and read for them even if your contracted time is over. This can get disruptive if people are disappointed, so here is how you deal with it: twenty minutes before you finish, find the host and tell them you are almost done. They might want to book you for more time so give them the option if you want to and are able. Then, choose the last person in line (as far out as twenty minutes–maybe the fourth person in line) and tell them that they are the last guest you will be reading for. Tell them to let people know who try to get into line behind them. Take good care of yourself and stop at the appointed time. Reading for more people to make them happy without getting paid only sets you up for burn-out and even resentment. Take care of your most precious resource: you!

Right Price

Pricing yourself is both an art and a science. There is a dance that you do with the host wherein they want to pay as little as possible and you want to make as much as you can. Hosts want to hire you for as little time as they can get away with, because you have an expensive rate (as you should!). To protect your energy, I suggest having working minimums. I have a two-hour minimum for any event, but I increase it to a three-hour minimum if it is a weekend event or has significant travel. For high demand weekends around

Halloween, I usually have a four-hour minimum for my services.

I've noticed that it's an industry standard to simply charge a per hour rate, but when we charge for parties in this way, we leave a lot of money on the table that could rightfully be ours. I encourage you to think in terms of submitting a unique quote for each event, rather than always going with the same hourly rate.

Think about it this way: should an event that is on a Saturday night around Halloween cost the same as a January Tuesday afternoon ladies' tea? As you become busier, it makes sense to look at your readings in terms of supply and demand. Also, keep in mind the travel aspect and the amount of time they are hiring you for. What if you say yes to a party on Halloween night that is an hour roundtrip and only two actual reading hours? The moment you say yes, there could be another client wanting to hire you for four hours and just right up the road. You can protect your energy and time by creating a dynamic quote system.

I construct my quotes starting with a base rate. Your base rate can vary depending on where you live, the economy, inflation, etc. As you become more successful, your base rate will likely rise. My base hourly rate increases depending on certain factors. For simplicity's sake, let's say $100 an hour is my base rate and $150 is my highest possible rate depending on those factors. Therefore, the quote fluctuates depending on the event:

- A weekend event (Friday-Sunday) adds fifteen dollars to the base rate.
- An evening event (after 5pm) adds another fifteen dollars.
- A fall event (September through December) adds twenty more dollars.

I also include travel time in the quote (*time* not distance) so I look at how long, with traffic, it would take me to get to and from the event. Any travel time below ten minutes is free. For math's sake, let's use fifty cents a minute as our travel cost.

Finally, I have a bulk discount based on total time reading. I give a ten percent discount for guests who book for four hours, twenty percent for five hours, and twenty-five percent for six hours or more.

Let's look at a scenario:

A museum wants to hire you for a four-hour, Halloween event on a Saturday night. Getting to the museum, with traffic, at that time it will take you thirty minutes one way and twenty minutes on the return. You can use an online map tool to see travel estimates for specific times of day.

So, your base rate is one hundred dollars an hour, but this event hits all of the special factors: it's on a weekend, in the evening, and during the peak fall season. The adjusted hourly rate is $150 per hour. This makes your quote $600 for the event. But when you factor in the 50 minutes of travel time, that adds another $25, raising the quote to $625. Finally, since they are also hiring you for a decent number of hours, you might want to give them a 10% bulk discount, lowering the cost of the 4 hours to $540. Your full quote, incorporating all of the peak factors, the discount, and the travel is $565.

You quote your hosts the amount of $565 for the scope of work which entails the reading time, already laid out (how many people you will read and for how long for each). If your host wishes to add time after hiring you, then you can offer extra hours at your reduced rate of $135 an hour. (This is your hourly rate of $150 with the bulk discount applied).

This might seem a bit complicated. Why not just have one price and be done with it? Because a varied system like this gives you a process that is consistent and keeps most variables in mind to make sure you are paid well for your time. If you start out with a system like this, it will grow with you and your business. For me, I make a good living just walking into my office and seeing clients one-to-one. If, let's say, I make $400 reading for 4 hours in my comfy office, why would I compete with myself and make less money for a party reading where there is travel, traffic, and tricky whisky drinking guests? The last thing I want to do it to spend time making less money. A party has to be, at minimum, commensurate with what I would normally make during my regular office hours. Ideally, it should net me even more.

Even if you are just starting out, you want to make sure that you feel amply compensated for working on a Saturday night, right? *Party reading is tough work, and you deserve to be paid adequately for it.*

Between Time

Time is of the essence in all situations. *Your most precious resource is time, not readings.* Since you are being paid for your time in total, and not just the amount that you are actively reading, keep this in mind when negotiating, and delivering readings.

My *preferred* rhythm is five guests per hour with ten-minute readings (though of course I can go much faster) This amount allows for an in-depth reading plus accounts for in-between time (the end of one reading and the beginning of the other). In-between time seems so inconsequential, what is a few minutes here and there? But it totally adds up and can wreck even the most carefully negotiated rate. There have been times where I've been tucked away on the third floor of a house and it could be three to five minutes between one guest leaving and the next one coming in. If you do not account for this in-between time, you'll find that you'll work for free because the host will hold you to reading for the number of people you agreed on, and she will not feel she has to pay you for extra!

I make it clear to the host that their guests need to be absolutely prompt for their readings, or it will begin to bite into their time. I keep my phone on so I can adjust the time as needed for each guest. This might mean that one guest will get the full ten minutes of the reading while a tardy guest gets eight minutes. *It's not your responsibility to stay at the event for free because people are not paying attention.* With adequate communication, and a keen eye on your watch, you'll be able to deliver on time.

Once, I had someone who wanted to book me fore an event at her house for my minimum time (two hours). This host had ten guests and she wanted a fifteen-minute reading for each. The math didn't add up (fifteen minutes each for ten guests is two and a half hours.) In order for me to meet her quota of ten guests with fifteen minutes each, she would have to purchase another thirty minutes. She didn't want to purchase an extra half hour, so she decided to cap the number to eight guests. Some hosts will be too casual, "Oh I don't know, eight to twelve guests." But you need to know how many people you'll read for so you can quote a decent amount of time and not be doing hurried back-room negotiations for more time at the event.

Often, hosts are thinking about their bottom line and not about what is actually possible for a tarot reader. It's your job to teach them. I had a bride-to-be inquire about booking me for her wedding reception. She wanted me to read for eighty people at five minutes each for three hours. She also wanted it done in such a way where I was not drawing people off of the dance floor (meaning I was not able to read for the entire time.) What she wanted was impossible.

Even with five-minute readings (let's add three minutes in-between to be on the safe side) we are looking at a max of twenty-two to twenty-five guests working at top speed with people getting incredibly short mini readings (guests tend to feel miffed if their readings are under five minutes). I also know that a tarot reader will pull people from the dance floor whether the host likes it or not. People often want readings more than they want to watch people wrestle for a bouquet.

I explained to her that she needed two readers in order to get close to what she was looking for. In the end, she decided not to book. She got a reality check about how this actually works. I would rather go back and forth to determine that what they want is impossible (and lose the gig) than promise something I know I cannot do. Most hosts have never actually hired a reader; it's not uncommon for their expectations to be unrealistic. It's important that you run the numbers and let them know what is possible. I would rather do this work up front so that I can weed out the hosts whose expectations mean we are not a good fit.

Format & Flow

The standard for reading tarot is to read for one person in private, or in a semi-private setting. Reading for guests via email, online or in-person usually means a one-to-one interaction. At public events, however, there may be a couple of friends listening in as part of the fun, so never assume a party reading is a private one unless you have agreed with the host on that kind of format. You might also decide that reading gallery style works for you. A psychic gallery is reading for an audience while you rove from table-to-table offering to read a few cards for the delight and amusement of the guests. (I talk about this in depth later.) Usually, however, I see guests one-to-one, tucked away in a quiet corner or in a separate room.

Over the Valentine holiday (another busy time for events), I had a husband who wanted to book a party reading for his wife. His wife requested a reader for her nine guests plus herself over two hours *à la* "Real Housewives reality TV style" in the main room as entertainment for the party. Apparently, on the show, a psychic was called in, much to the delight and drama of TV ratings. Normally, for gallery readings there is a larger number of people, or there is a shorter time frame (perhaps as quick as five minutes). So, ten minutes for each guest in front of others can be uncomfortably intimate.

After we talked, I googled "Housewives and psychic" and the results terrified me. There was no way I wanted to be part of any philandering husband reveals in a group format or a cat fight that a psychic kicks off. It seemed to me that there was not one kind, gentle, or loving Housewives episode where a psychic came calling. If these are the examples that the wife was basing her hopes on, then I want to protect the other guests as much as myself.

I pushed back on the format with my host. I told him that it would be best to have small, private sessions with each guest. I find that in house-based parties, it's particularly important to aim for privacy. There are always family and friend dynamics that are in play in ways that public venues do not have. I explained all of this to the husband.

The husband contacted me to sheepishly explain how adamant his wife was on this style of reading despite my suggestion. By then, a feeling of anxiety appeared in my gut. I listened to my intuition about the situation and told him that they could follow the format that I was suggesting, or they could find a reader that might be better suited to what she wanted. The husband, who by now was only three days to the event (woe to last minute planners), ended up taking my suggestion. The party went beautifully, and the wife was effusive of her praise at the end. They didn't miss a thing.

I share this story because you might be asked to do things that are not within your comfort zone, and it's totally okay to say no. *If it does not feel right, kindly decline.* You are the professional. When you honor your boundaries, they will keep you happy and safe.

Make sure that you are clear on whatever kind of format you are comfortable with when negotiating a party, especially a house party. Readings in a home can be particularly tricky because you are not on neutral ground. You are walking into someone else's castle, and their dynamics, histories and hidden motives can certainly affect your work. Ensure that you are communicating effectively enough so that everyone is on the same page.

3
Dancing in the Dark
Make friends with Ambiguity and Uncertainty

House Parties

House parties are where most public readers get started. There are two types of house party: hosted and non-hosted. In a hosted party, the host is paying you directly at a per-hour rate, and the guests are not paying anything. A non-hosted party is one where the host is supplying the place for the party, but each guest is paying you individually for their reading.

Even though a house party is fairly casual, you still need to give it professional treatment. You need a contract and should consider including disclosures for everyone to sign before you begin reading. It's a crazy litigious world out there, so I want to cover my risks as much as I possibly can. In my day practice, all guests must read and agree to my disclaimer as part of the onboarding process. I also have business liability insurance. I will talk more about this later, and I have a sample document that you are free to use for your own events.

Once you have agreed with your host, and the negotiations are over, I recommend a deposit to hold the time slot. Every time I've not requested a deposit, I have come to regret it. It's no fun to have a huge Halloween party cancel on you one week before Halloween and you are left scrambling to find a replacement after turning down ten other invitations. As much as you may feel a spiritual purpose in doing this work, always remember that money talks! What if that cancellation means you couldn't take another job? There goes the rent! It's no biggie to them, but it could potentially be a huge deal for you.

Make sure to tell your host that the time and date is not reserved until you have a deposit in your hot, little hands. The deposit can vary. I usually only require a fifty-dollar deposit which is refundable up to two weeks prior to the event. But for fall events the deposit is a nonrefundable fifty percent of the ticket. I only accept cash, debit or credit, or payment through the app of my choice. I don't accept private checks. Some readers I know also accept Money Orders or Certified Checks for private events. This is a smart move because like cash, once it is in your hand, it is yours. For non-hosted events, the host can either put that money towards her reading, or she will have it reimbursed to her on the day of the party, provided that the number of guests and everything you agreed upon is still in place.

Non-Hosted Events

A non-hosted party is a gig situation where the host is not paying you for readings but rather acts as coordinator. She is lining up her guests and providing the space, but each individual you read for will be paying for their own time with you. A non-hosted party is often the choice for readers who are within their first year and are trying to build their client base. A non-hosted party is tricky because no one is paying you for in-between time, and you can easily find yourself with a loss of thirty minutes or more because no one is in a rush to see you!

Another challenge is that the host does not feel pressure to make sure that the number of guests you both agreed on will be there when you show up. Let's say you agreed to read for fifteen people over three hours, but once you arrive it's a different story.

Perhaps the host says that she couldn't get fifteen, and that she only has six people, but she still expects you to stay and read for them. *Tell the hostess to agree on a minimum guarantee to book. If she is unable to hit that minimum on the day of the party, then she is still responsible for covering the amount you both agreed upon.* With her money on the table, believe me, this is the motivation she needs to ensure that the number of guests you agreed on will be there!

Hired Help

Some hosts are solicitous. They will stop by a number of times to ensure your drink is filled or offer you something to eat. Others will invite you to stay and enjoy the party. Good hosts will be mindful of the guests coming to your table and will pay you promptly when your time is up. I love these wonderful, thoughtful hosts: may they live a long and happy life!

As friendly and welcoming as a good host might be, never lose sight that you are under their employ and are working (not attending) their party. While a host might offer you cocktails, a plate of food, or an offer to stay and enjoy, it's usually a bad idea to accept. For one, I never have time to eat while I'm reading at a party, and if I did, it looks devastatingly unprofessional to eat a platter at your reading table. For obvious reasons, you don't want to enjoy those cocktails.

Finally, if you hang around at the house after you're done, it can be awkward. Perhaps you talked about a guest's divorce or a recent job change, and now you are clinking glasses with them? Trust me, it never goes well. The intimacy of the tarot table does not easily translate to any other intimacy. People will feel uncomfortable about the new role you are now playing, especially if they divulged something intimate with you before! Work to maintain that sense of safety with them. Stay in your lane.

Freebie Fifteen

This has become an often-enough phenomena that I've come to expect it. Usually, a host is so busy that they won't have time, to get a reading from you. As the host stops by to pay you at the end of your time, they will mention how they never had a chance to get a reading. This is the only occasion that I will go over my allotted time without compensation. If the host who hired me didn't get a reading, I want to make sure that she gets one. Hosts are going to be your biggest supporters and believers, and they will often hire you for other parties. So, you want to keep them happy.*Remember, this is the exception to the rule - so only one freebie allowed.* After that, make a quick exit if you can or negotiate a rate to stay.

Rotten Hosts

Do this work long enough and even with the best contract, you'll encounter a bad host. I have some horror stories—tales from the tarot trenches, if you will. I've learned to carry water with me because hosts leave and never check up again. Some hosts might make you play the "heavy" and will not back you up when it's time for you to leave, forcing you to tell the guests that your time is over. Your host might decide that they want to change the contract, or stiff you in pay or do any kind of malicious things. This is why it's important to never forget that you are hired entertainment. Stay on your toes and take care of yourself because you are going into homes that can run the gamut between wonderful and miserable. Make sure that you bring a physical copy of your contract and have your host check over all of it and verbally agree with you one more time before you begin. That helps for any "misunderstandings" that might occur at the end of your night.

Once, I worked a bachelorette party that was quite a distance from my location, but I was happy to do it because they were paying for five hours. When I got there, the bride-to-be installed me in a bedroom in her parents' affluent home. Over the period of five hours I proceeded to read for fifteen of her guests for twenty minutes each, all back-to-back. I know I knocked it out of the park, my readings were particularly good that night, and the guests were all amazed by their readings.

Despite how hard I worked, not once did the hostess or her maid of honor check in or offer me anything to drink. In five hours, I left once to quickly use the bathroom. At the end of my long shift as I packed up to leave the bride (who was quite drunk) pulled out the contract: I had made a mistake on it and accidentally put a figure that was twenty dollars less than what I quoted her in the email. She intended to make me stick to the contract, knowing full well it was less than what I quoted her. I told her that it was an error, and that I am to be paid the rate I quoted her. She dug in her heels, and so did I. I was not feeling magnanimous. Her maid of honor, seeing the situation through sober eyes, pulled the bride-to-be into a separate bedroom. I could hear them arguing, but at the end of it the maid of honor came out and gave me the full amount including a tip.

Because of that experience, I now triple check my contract and bring a physical copy with me. Some readers ask for payment up front, but I don't, I would rather settle at the end in case they book me for more time. Every difficult host teaches me an invaluable lesson. They make me a better business person.

Happy Hour

 A couple of years ago, I hit upon an idea where I play the host for tarot parties. This is only possible because I have an office and waiting room. I offer thirty-minute readings for a party of four to six guests, including wine and nonalcoholic beverages, savory and sweet snacks, and a lovely, candle-lit atmosphere. My guests enjoy hanging out with their friends until it's their turn to receive their reading.

I really enjoy hosting these Tarot Happy Hours because it allows me to scale my service. Each guest is paying my standard rate for a reading including a premium for the beverages and food. I do not have to travel to them and can read, at my best, in the comfort of my own office. Plus, none of the guests have to worry about hosting. They can come and have a good time and leave while I do the clean-up. If you have the space, you might want to consider this option. Even though they are coming to me, I still require a deposit and contract. There are never any exceptions to this rule.

Public Events

I do more public events of than any other type of party. Public events are gigs where you are still being hired by a private person, but the location is not in a private home. You could be going to a public venue like a wedding hall, a restaurant, or catering hall. Sometimes there is an open bar, a photo booth, and a DJ. The event could be a wedding, a bar mitzvah or a 50th birthday party.

Many events will have people of all ages attending, so now is a good time to determine whether you'll read for children and, if so, whether you have a cut-off age. At house parties, you are the main attraction, and everyone works around you, but at public events, you are a side attraction. As the side attraction, you might have to stop while someone gives a speech or cuts a cake. Because of the nature of public events, there is usually no hard guest number but rather a ballpark you need to hit within the guest number. Since you are there for atmosphere, your readings need to be more entertainment-minded than the typical house party. We do not need Jane at her 40th birthday party told her husband is thinking about divorcing her, do we?

Spatial Needs

The biggest challenge with public events is spatial. You'll be working with odd spaces, so you have to be particularly clear about your needs. Hosts have no idea, in general, what you are going to need. They are thinking about traffic and flow in deciding where to place you and are not necessarily thinking about privacy of their guests or whether it's quiet enough so that you don't lose your voice. The last part is particularly important: talking in a loud party as a guest is nothing like the constant speaking you'll need to do for hours on end. You'll lose your voice if the space you are working in is too loud.

Because the host doesn't understand your particular needs, you might be wedged next to the waiter's station or placed next to a live band or DJ. The table and chair may be woefully inadequate to your needs. This is where your fifteen-minute set-up time comes into play. Despite your best efforts, you might have to make adjustments to your location once you arrive. Please don't be afraid to advocate for yourself. I have portable furniture that is comfortable for working which I offer to bring as part of the service. I do not enjoy going to the chiropractor after spending five hours bent over a low coffee table while reading cards. As a tarot reader doing public work, you are at risk for repetitive injuries. You won't be getting workers comp if you throw out your back, so speak up.

There was one event in particular that was being hosted at a banquet hall in a restaurant and so I assumed that the furniture wouldn't be a problem. However, when I got there, they had stationed me at a high bistro table (you know the kind you might find in a busy bar). It was suitable for holding a drink or two but not much else. I explained that I cannot stand for hours at the table like this and that the table was far too small for doing readings. I needed enough room to spread my cards out, and I also want to be able to put my promotional materials out.

Even with that stressful beginning, I was able to work with the venue manager to create an area much more conducive for readings. I even helped them bring out chairs and a very heavy table, but it was worth it and set a much better atmosphere for the busy evening ahead. My mistake was not reaching out to the venue beforehand to express my needs. That's why it makes sense to talk to the manager to ensure you have everything you need on hand and ready to go.

Buddy System

At public events you might find yourself working alongside caterers, bartenders, musicians, other psychics, magicians, or actors. These folks will often be the most important people for you to get to know. They can assist you by watching your line so you can use the restroom. They might bring you a snack for your break, or just stop by to make sure that your drink is filled. They will watch out for you when the host is too busy. Most caterers and other service professionals are not allowed to get a reading with you, but they are often the folks who grab my business card and make an appointment later. If time allows, and if they can, giving them a quick reading does a lot to foster goodwill. Treat your comrades well.

Corporate Events

Corporate events are gigs where you are being hired directly by a company. These can range from small- to mid-sized companies like a hair salon or a real estate business to big-name corporations like clothing design firms, famous museums, and large retail stores. (Fun fact, my weirdest corporate gig was reading at a grocery store, I was next to the bananas. Coincidence? I think not!)

Typically, you'll work with the HR person or the administrative assistant of the boss. Sometimes they have an event planner, and you'll work through them. You will most likely talk to someone who is tasked with reaching out to several readers for their event. These people are looking for price, professionalism, and availability. They will then report their intel gathering to someone else—usually the person who will be making the decision to hire you.

Always follow up on these initial conversations with a strong proposal letter. When you do, it gives the person you talked to a document that they can pass on to the decision maker. Your goal is to get the decision maker to decide upon you, and a proposal letter will give you the kind of exposure that an initial phone call will not. Your proposal letter needs to reflect *their* level of professionalism but include *your* persuasive language. Think of this a "cover letter" for corporate gigs!

Matching the tone of a corporate event means being prompt with replies, creating a proposal letter that is persuasive and giving them an attractive quote. You know, corporate style. Usually, they will take a fine-tooth comb to your contract and will pay by check (though sometimes I will take a company credit card over the phone). Some corporate events will require you to purchase your own event and liability coverage or ask that you put their name under yours on your policy.

For corporate events you are usually being hired for one of two reasons: as a promotional draw to bring people to their event or as a benefit to their employees. If you are being hired as a promotional entertainer, you'll be working with their guests, so your readings and look need to have a fine polish. No upsetting readings here; these must be treated carefully. Corporate headquarters will take issue with upset clients. Bring your lightest touch to these promotional events.

If you are hired for internal use, the atmosphere tends to be more relaxed. I've worked with a number of companies in the restaurant industry who hold their holiday parties in February because they are usually too busy working over the holiday season themselves. In my experience, employees tend to be on their best behavior for readings. They have not forgotten that their boss is just on the other side of the pasta station, so you'll usually have no problems with these guests. They do not over drink, but they will be more skeptical on the whole. You might find that they'll want to "test" you more than other gigs.

In both cases, I find I work the easiest in corporate gigs. I will actually have slow spots during these events. Usually they are not counting the minutes or the number of people being read for. Corporate events let me leave at the appointed time, on the dot, and will pay me promptly if not ahead of time.

Tip Me

Gratuities can be a nice addition to the income you are making, but they have their time and place. I don't put a gratuity jar out for private events (house parties or weddings,) but I often do at public and corporate events (where the guests aren't paying and the venue is large). *It's perfectly okay to ask!* However, I never put a tip jar out without host permission. I did a gig once that was sponsored by a beer company; it was on a boat and the mood was festive. The guests were mostly bartenders and servers who know the value of tipping. At the end of three hours I made an additional $120 in tips on top of the hourly rate I negotiated.

Event Companies

Event companies work as middle men to pull together events such as high-end weddings, big ticket name corporate venues, and events that are large. I have to be honest with you, working with event companies is my least favorite format of party work. I prefer to work for myself. The anti-authoritarian in me chafes a bit at other people's rules. Even though the wage you get through them will be lower than what you alone could negotiate, they can make up in volume what they might lack in rate. Also, they will expose you to events that you might not otherwise be able to attend.

Similar to reaching out to women-owned businesses in the *Get Booked* section, you can also pound the pavement in this area. Use Google to find event companies near you and call the office to introduce yourself. For this approach, I find that a phone call is more effective than an email. Offer to do a *pro bono* tarot reading lunch hour for their staff or show up to the office with a professional letter of intent along with your promotional materials. You can also follow event companies on social media from your own tarot accounts, so they get a sense of who you are. Basically, let them know you exist.

There are also event company professional organizations where you can meet these business owners and ply your trade. In the US, here are just a few that might be worth your time to investigate:

ILEA: International Live Events Association
NACE: National Association for Catering and Events
MPI: Meetings Professionals International
ICCA: International Congress and Convention Association

CEMA: Corporate Event Marketing Association

ILEA and NACE were coordinating an annual luncheon for stakeholders on a boat a few years ago. Guess who showed up with a fake parrot on her shoulder and gave free readings? This gal did! While I was there, I literally wallpapered these people with my card and got some really nice gigs. This technique requires a lot of schmoozing and chutzpah (internal fortitude) to pull off well. But when you do, the rewards are worth it.

It's not uncommon for an event coordinator to prohibit your business card or promotional materials on site. Event companies work hard to market and secure contracts, so if you take a company from them, it's considered poaching, and that is bad form. Also, they may limit your direct access to the company because they do not want you to undercut them. Fair enough. I completely understand why an event company that works hard to secure contracts would hate for little old me to come along and rob them of their cut!

Often event companies will furnish you with their own contract, code of conduct, and will tell you what to wear and what to do. For US based readers, these companies will also require a W9 (this is the tax form for freelance workers). Your income will be reported to the IRS from their end via the W9. It is important to keep track of paperwork in order to claim this income on your tax forms. Also, in the US, you'll most likely be housed under their liability insurance, so you do not have to get your own, whereas in other countries, the event company will want you to carry your own.

If, like me, you have an independent streak, you might find working with event companies to be a bit confining. However, when you work with them you know you are getting the money, and you know you are working with a reputable company. When your time ends, you are done. There is no tipsy host who wants you to stay longer, and there are no issues with getting paid at the end of the night. This piece of mind can be absolutely worth the control they will exert over the process.

Devilish Details

Outlined here are the kinds of paperwork you will see or create as a professional party reader. As they are all samples from my own collection and particular expertise, I encourage you to do further research in your area to create documents that will fit your needs and location. Copies of each are included in the appendix.

Proposal: A proposal is a formalized quote for the scope of work for a potential employer. Make sure you are including travel reimbursement, parking costs, or anything else that might be above your normal rate. I tend to add some marketing language as to why they should hire me, and I may throw in a review or two from previous clients. I use the biggest names possible or choose a review from a company that is similar to the one I'm negotiating with.

Party Contract: Once a client has decided to hire you, you'll need to send them a contract. The contract will outline the agreement such as amount, date, venue, length of time, breaks, and what you will need as a reader. The contract will state financial details already transacted, like a deposit plus what is still owed. The contract includes language about what to do when a dispute arises and agreements that protect you from liability. I recommend hiring a lawyer to draw up an event contract template for your business so that it conforms to the applicable laws in your area. *Do not confirm any event until you have both the contract signed and the deposit in your hand.* Do not agree to any gig without a contract even if they are your best friend in all the world. If you forget just everything else in this book, please remember this one. You need a contract!

Host Letter: This Host Letter is part of the work in training your host. You know by now from reading my many stories here that hosts are by-and-large clueless about what you need. Never assume they know anything about hosting you, so spell it out for them in writing. My host letter includes what I will typically need as a reader and also what I can and cannot do in simple language. For example, if you are not a medium, clearly state such. Guests may have no idea that there are differences between us intuitive entertainers. Lay out your expectations and limitations ahead of time so no one is disappointed. Send this document out the week of the event and ask the host if they have any questions. I like to include "what to expect" information for the host to share with other guests, if they feel called to do so.

Liability Insurance: I carry liability insurance that covers both standard liability (slips and falls) and professional liability (errors and omissions). If someone slips and falls because they tripped on my rug or feels that what I told them harmed them and decides to sue me, my insurance will pay for my representation in civil court. In the US it is extremely difficult to find an insurance policy that will cover a tarot card reader; however, there are a few companies out there that will.

I hesitate to share this because I fear that as soon as I do, the information will be obsolete. But as of this writing there are two insurance companies that have underwritten for me as a tarot professional in the US. They are Hiscox business insurance and Alternative Balance. You can look them up yourself to determine whether their coverage limits and pricing is within your own particular needs.

Some event companies have their own liability insurance which is extended to their contractors while others will require that you carry your own. I've mentioned it before but it bears repeating, some corporate events will not book you until you actually add their name to your policy of coverage. I pay about $250 a year for my policy, and it is the perfect amount of money that allows me to sleep like a baby at night. Between this and the disclaimer, I feel as legally protected as I can be.

Event Company Contract: While not included in the appendix because this will vary from company to company, keep in mind that you are likely to encounter contracts written by the event company that they expect you to sign and adhere to. Do not presume that their contract is fair. If anything, you should assume that a company's contract is focused on their own interests. Be prepared to read over it when you get it and ask questions if there are things you do not understand or wish to renegotiate. Always remember that contracts are malleable until they are signed.

Blank W9: I mention the W9 form again but it is very important. If you are in the US and you are hired by a company, they will require you to fill out and return a W9. Fully expect that they will report to the IRS that they paid you. You'll need to claim income made from this event at tax time. Failure to do so may mean tax trouble for you. I keep one of these signed and scanned each year to easily send off to any company that requires it.

Disclaimer: While nearly impossible to conduct in large events, you can have individuals sign a disclaimer for house parties. Some professional readers do not agree to this practice, saying that it will not hold up in court should you run into trouble. Since there is no legal precedent that I know of as to whether a disclaimer would hold up in court or not, I prefer to be safe than sorry.

I like the disclaimer because the person signing it is absolutely clear on the scope of your responsibilities. I think it sets up expectations for better behavior. If I can make copies that people sign at the beginning of the night, why not? As with the contract, you may want to work with a lawyer to create a disclaimer that is in accordance with your local laws and governance. I do include a sample in the appendix.

Party Sales Receipt: I usually email a receipt the day after the event. I do not bring it to the party because the gig can change, and the final charge might be different than what we originally agreed on. This is also my chance to personally thank them once again for hiring me.

Real Cards: I add this because I think it's a nice touch. I send thank you and holiday cards to hosts that I had a good experience with. I will even include a nice tarot card from a broken deck plus one of my business cards. Whenever possible, I'm trying to build a relationship, and I want them to think about hiring me again in the future. In a society that is so transactional, where there are few to any social niceties in correspondence, where ghosting is the norm, I want to take a more careful, care-filled and cultivated approach when building relationships to my clients. They are important to me. They allow me to do this work, and I get to be of service in a profound way. I want them to know how important they are to me.

If you are new to running your own business, I know that paperwork (especially the legal stuff) can be intimidating. Embrace the paperwork, my friend, as it's the only thing truly protecting you should things go awry. As you may remember from my story previously, I mistyped an amount by twenty dollars and the hostess fully intended on not paying what she knew was the verbally agreed upon price. Triple check your work, do not assume that "good intentions" will save the day. Some events will want you to "courtesy hold" dates (and then will drop you after you were kindly blocking out a date for them) or expect you to show up day of and then sign the contract. No way. They either hold to your process, or they can find someone else.

4
It's Go Time
When the Deck Hits the Table

Massive Bandwidth

I charge more per hour for event readings than I do in my regular practice because party work is so demanding. Party readings require an incredible amount of mental effort to pull off well. Mentally, I'm processing three different levels of awareness. On the first level, I'm conducting the reading itself—which is no small feat. The second level is logistics, timing, and making sure that I'm staying exactly on-point with my time markers, "Okay, I have five minutes left and six cards. How do I do this in the allotted time?" The third level is social consciousness, "How is this person responding to what I'm saying? Are they processing the information? Are they enjoying themselves?" It's easy to see how we can often feel both exhilarated from the high of giving many readings and exhausted at the same time.

It's not uncommon, especially in the beginning, to need a day off after doing a party because of the sheer energy that is required to do them. I've heard of some readers who are never tired because they take energy from the Universe. They simply allow the guest's energy flow through them. While I'm happy they have limitless energy, if you are exhausted the next day, it's because you worked hard, and you deserve the break. Treat your body well and, with time, you'll gain endurance for party readings.

Self-Care

You cannot be a strong professional reader if you don't take care of yourself. Self-care means taking your needs seriously—even if other people don't understand. Self-care requires a loving dedication to yourself as the driver of your own happiness and well-being. Caring for yourself means planning ahead for your needs. It also means saying no if you need to. Self-care is not indulgent or selfish; when you care for yourself you are a better reader and a better business owner. Nurturing yourself is the vanguard protecting us from burnout and exhaustion which can lead to giving bad readings.

It's important that your rituals for self-care take place not only before the event, but through it as well. In fact, the way you care for yourself while you are reading will determine how well you do, how you feel, and whether you will be booked again. Consider these aspects of nurturing yourself and plan accordingly. You are important. Repeat after me: "I am important."

Repetitive Motion

About a year into my tarot career, I was working a lot of gigs. Around the same time, my elbow began hurting, and I could not for the life of me figure out what I did to it. Painkillers and analgesic rubs were not cutting the mustard, and I was in constant pain. I eventually figured out *that I had developed tennis elbow from all the shuffling!* This is a common injury for tarot readers. What healed my elbow was a TheraBand flex bar. You can buy one online for under twenty dollars. I used it every day to build muscles around the area, and I never had any problems since.

Party readers are particularly prone to repetitive motion injuries in their arms, hands, fingers and backs. Not every situation will have a table at waist height with appropriate chairs for you to sit in a comfortable position with your feet on the floor. I am often twisted to the side in loud events so I can speak into people's ears or find the table not as perfect as I would like. As much as this is a cognitive job, it is also a surprisingly physical one, as well.

Liquid Effects

Real talk: my bladder is probably the size of a walnut! Hydration and bathroom logistics are exceedingly important to me! As a rule, you'll be talking a lot which means you'll be drinking to soothe your throat—especially when you are in a loud location. Since you'll be drinking a lot, yo'll probably need to use the restroom more than usual. Stipulate in your contract that you are entitled to a bathroom break. I suggest one every two hours. Take this bathroom break whether you really feel the need to go or not. It can be hard to take breaks because people will pressure you to keep reading in some situations. Don't let anyone talk you into sacrificing your own basic needs just so you can read for one more person.

There may be a line to the bathroom at large events. Often, I only have a five- or ten-minute break, and I cannot afford to wait in line before needing to get back to my table. First, I ask a caterer or other event professional if there is a service bathroom in the kitchen or somewhere where the guests are not welcome. If there isn't, I will actually ask the first person in line if I can cut and explain the situation. Usually, people are quite generous when they know you have to get back to your table ASAP.

Line Management

Managing the line can be tricky. Some hosts will do the work ahead of time and give you a list of names and times so everyone knows exactly when to show up. I really enjoy a nice orderly procession of people, but this system does have its challenges because sometimes I'm expected to find the next guest on my list. As we have discussed, in-between time can really affect your ability to finish the event on time! If I am in a hurry, I'll have the guest I just read for go searching for the next person on the list. Hopefully your host understands that you need her to have each person ready to go right on the dot, and if she doesn't, the guest will get whatever time is left after their late arrival.

If you are working a large venue and the space is oddly shaped, it might be hard for a line to form naturally. When this is the case, people will arrive in a way that I describe as "popcorn style." By that, I mean that people are milling about in different locations and distances from your table. It will not be clear to you who is waiting, much less who is first. This is a challenging set-up because you'll be busy conducting readings and might not have much bandwidth to figure out who is next.

People take their turns seriously and will confront anyone they think is cutting the line. They will expect you to mediate the dispute, but if you are busy reading, this can cause a far bigger issue than you wish to deal with. As much as humanely possible, have a line-like system set-up with the host before you begin reading. You may even want to pack a small dry erase board so you can write out, "Line Starts Here" and place it on a chair a few feet away from your table.

If there is still a line when your contracted time is up, do not extend your time even if you are doing quick readings. People always want to ask one more question, sit a little longer, flirt with you, or ask about how tarot works. If your guests are curious and intrigued–in fact I take it as a compliment when people say that my readings are weird, or "really creepy"– you are doing a great job. However, the people waiting in line will absolutely know if you are giving one person more time than another. There is no quicker way to anger a mob of waiting people than by being inconsistent in this area.

Additionally, if you are working with another reader, make an agreement with them about the time that you each are going to mind for each client. If they are being inconsistent and slow while you are working efficiently, people will ask you, "Why does he give them more time?"

Keep in mind, *there is an inverse relationship between a guest's patience and the number of drinks they've had*. You have to be quite strict about this, I'm afraid, and if you are asked to extend your time, say no. If they want more questions answered, they can get back in line or take your card. Use a timer if you need one.

I've had hosts literally gesture to me to "make it faster" to get more people in, but I hold my ground. The absolute fastest I can do a reading is 5 minutes. That includes shuffling the cards, the guest asking their question and picking cards, and my reading. Anything less than this and people will start to feel like they waited in line only to be cheated out of something meaningful. I stand by my process; I will not allow the host or anyone else to bully me into subpar performance due to their unrealistic expectations.

Your Table

I've read on coffee tables, lawyer's desks, card tables, and just about everything in between. I've tossed tarot at the corner of a conference room table and on basically every single strange configuration of table you can think of. Because I'm not usually updated about the table type before I show up, I keep my table decorations pretty simple and modifiable. I have three black tablecloths (square, rectangle and round) along with a table runner where I lay my cards. I will typically use some combination of these, and, at minimum, I will use a spread cloth to protect my cards. Often, I don't need my own tablecloths as the host will have created a pretty table for me, but I always bring them just in case.

My tablecloth and runner are in white, silver, and black. These colors will match well with most décor schemes. I have a silver dish for business cards, a tip jar (when appropriate), a candle, and occasionally some stones if I feel like packing them. My party set-up is simple and elegant and able to match just about any conditions. Because I'm often uncertain about venue or parking, I try to keep my party bag as light as possible.

For breaks, make sure you take your tips with you. Also, you might want to wrap up your deck and take it along, too. You might find that if you leave your deck it could be gone when you return, or you will find guests sitting in your chair playing fortune teller with your cards.

Fashion Plate

Since my table is decorated in black and silver, I tend to wear mostly black for every event unless we agreed to a costume or some other kind of outfit. I have black cocktail dresses and black hippie skirts. I have black laced items rivaling Stevie Nicks of Fleetwood Mac on a good day, black sheath dresses, and just about everything in between. While the style may change, the color usually does not.

The reason why I chose black is that it always looks basically nice and is the most versatile for most types of events (except maybe weddings or bridal events). Also, in large venues, other workers such as wait staff, caterers, and bartenders all wear black, and since I'm also a party hire, I conform to this unspoken standard. It has the added benefit of alerting the staff that you are also a staff person like themselves. For event gigs, I have so many things to keep in mind that when I can take the issue of wardrobe choice off the list, I arrive in a calmer state because I wasn't stressing out about what to wear.

Keep in mind, this is just my personal preference based on negating my own preparation anxieties. I know other readers who truly excel at putting effort into their wardrobe; their party garb is vibrant and entertaining. In this area: you do you!

Lastly, you may want to reconsider requests that ask you to dress as a 'Gypsy Fortuneteller'. I personally find that the costume is a form of cultural appropriation that I am not comfortable with. Some people also take issue with the word gypsy, as it refers to people who call themselves Travelers, or the Roma and is considered a slur by some.

I am not comfortable donning a cultural artifact that is only loosely aligned with a people and its culture. There are many other costumes I can happily wear (and love buying because I get to write costumes off as tax expense, win!). I don't need to perpetuate the baggage associated with the 'Gypsy Fortuneteller' label.

Auditory Warning

Noise is number one on my list of challenges as a party reader. Hosts do not understand that, while reading, you are constantly talking at a volume and pace far above the casual conversations around you at the party. You have to talk loud enough for the guest who is hanging onto every word you say. Raising the ambient noise even just a little bit affects your ability to speak for hours at a time. Add a band or a DJ to that background noise and you have to get even louder to be heard.

When it's particularly loud, I will pull the guest's chair directly next to mine (rather than across the table) so I can speak into their ear. Encourage them to sit close; the closer they are the quieter you can be. I have plenty of throat lozenges on hand to soothe my throat, and I use ear plugs if the din is particularly loud. I have it on good authority from a voice coach/tarot reader that mint and menthol will dry out your throat tissue. Opt for fruit lozenges, instead. If it's unbearable, I will ask the host to move me somewhere else. Even with the best communication in the world, the host is focused on the party, not your comfort, so when you get to your designated spot, look to where possible sources of noise might come from. If it looks too close for comfort, ask to be moved elsewhere.

There is a tricky spatial calculation in that the host wants you to be seen so people can mosey over but being seen might also mean reading in a loud location. Work with your host to find something appropriate for you but know that one of the occupational hazards to this service is an occasional loss of voice. Sadly, I do not have the magic answer to this vexing issue as a party reader. The best I can do is give you a heads-up on this particular challenge so that can be aware and do the best you can and have a nice cup of ginger tea, after.

Draw the Line

Your boundaries as a party reader will be unique to you. There is no right or wrong way to have them. One reader will tolerate and enjoy a rowdier party while another reader will require a calm environment. Boundaries are just parameters you set to support your ability to be at your best. You may have transportation or mobility issues and will need special accommodations. You may not be comfortable working in a bar or late at night. Thinking about where your boundaries are and being able to say no to what isn't a fit is the hallmark of a professional.

One of my personal issues is night driving. I manage chronic migraines, so night driving—especially when there are bright headlights—is a major trigger for me. If the location is dark and in a place that I'm not familiar with, there may be some special accommodations I need to keep in mind such as getting a ride or using a ride share service. I may not take a gig if I find this will particularly challenge my condition. Whenever possible, though, I make accommodation instead of letting my condition stop me from doing the work.

At some house parties, everyone stays over slumber-party style. They may not be concerned about the weather, but you are looking out the window wondering how high the snow will be and whether you can get home. Or, you might be coming from a distance and the sky just opened up outside, right as you finish. You may consider including an "inclement weather policy" in your contract. One of my tarot colleagues, Christiana Gaudet, has set up a video chat with her in a private room. Location and weather is irrelevant if there is Wi-Fi; she is able to attend a party even if there is a blizzard is happening but she will be online.

Safety First

If you arrive at an event and you feel unsafe, you do not have to stay at the event. Period. I don't care how mad the host and party guests will get. Your safety and comfort are paramount. Party readings are a risk. As much as you might be able to vet an organization and their location, you honestly do not know what you are walking into until you get there. Hopefully, the background work you have done means you are working in a professional setting, but at the end of the day, when drinks are flowing and you are in someone else's home or venue or business, you can only control so much.

Here is what I do to manage my own safety. First, I let my partner know where I'm going: the address, the time I should be there, host contact information and any other relevant data. If my partner doesn't hear from me after fifteen minutes of the end of my time, he will call me. If I do not respond within ten minutes after that, he will call the host. If the host is unreachable and the venue is close, he will come to the event location. If the event is too far, then he then will call the police. Thankfully, the last two options have never happened, and hopefully they never will. In any event, a safety protocol needs to be put in place at any time you are in a new location.

In my early days I went to a party for a woman's 50th birthday celebration. Her husband hired me and put me in a private office with a separate entrance while the revelers were outside in the garden. I dressed in my "renaissance garb" as I was asked to come in costume. I tried to lace my bodice loosely because I didn't think it would do to be "all out there" over my tarot table! The party became absolute pandemonium. Let's just say the god Bacchus was influencing this crowd!

Towards the end of the evening, two men that I had read for earlier came into my room while I was packing up. They were drunk, and I knew instantly by the way they were towering over me that they had intentions other than getting a reading. They both kept saying how "cute" I was and how nice that bodice looked on me. It was one of the most potentially dangerous situations I have ever been in as a reader. At the time, I just scrambled out of their way as fast as I could and ran to the host to get my payment. I asked him to escort me back to the room to get my things and then to walk me to the car. Even as I was trying to leave, the drunk men were trying to get me to stay—to the point where they blocked the sidewalk path. The host had to push them out of the way so I could leave.

As a rule, and for the above reasons, I find house parties to be the most dangerous. People are in a domestic setting and are usually drinking more than they would in public. People feel comfortable in their own settings and might take liberties they never would in a public space. I share this story with you to reiterate how important your safety is, how important it is to have a plan in place, should a situation like this arise. Let people know where you will be and when you will be done. Keep in mind your own level of comfort, and don't assume that everyone is well intentioned. Be careful, my friend, and maintain your boundaries.

Drinking & Reading

There is definitely a split camp on the question of whether "to drink or not to drink" in the professional tarot world. Some readers feel that any kind of drinking during a reading impacts their abilities. Others have no problem having a drink or two. Personally, I've done both depending on how I feel. A glass of wine as I begin my night is a great way to relax any anxiety I might feel. Of course, I never overindulge (one drink only) and I take my cues from the host. If the host offers a drink and I feel like it, I may accept. If the host does not offer a drink, then I never ask for one. In general, I feel out the atmosphere of the party and take my cue from there.

Bad Actors

Corporate and public events will typically have a higher than average number of skeptics. These people will feel the need to test you. You will run into people at these events who won't respect you. These guests would never buy a reading from you, but since you are there, why not toy with you so they can feel superior? This, honestly, is the biggest downside of party readings. While you need to deal with them, do not let the five percent stop you from reading when the other ninety-five percent are amazing people.

Often, this difficult five percent will be the result of one-too-many drinks. The later it gets, the more this becomes an issue to deal with. When people drink, their social niceties diminish. I've been to parties where I was the only sober one in attendance. When it comes to alcohol, you need to decide what your cut off point is. In my contract I state that I have the right to refuse anyone who is inebriated. When I do get a person who has had one too many, I tell them that I'm unable to get a reading because their energy is not clear. Usually, that is a sufficient answer.

Very early on in my career I worked a house party where everyone was very drunk. One woman passed out at the table while I was trying to give her a reading! When I woke her up, she tried to leave by going between my table and the wall. In her state, she didn't see that I was charging my phone, and she close-lined herself on my charger. My phone went flying across the room! Luckily, my phone was undamaged. Did I end the job then and there? I didn't, but I should have. I took the abuse because I didn't want to cause a problem. Looking back, I can't believe how I allowed myself to be treated.

Mandatory Choices

Party readings tend to require a more predictive style. At a party, people are usually not too interested in the deep personal and spiritual analysis that tarot can reveal (there are always fun outliers, though!). Typically, people are looking for two things: a psychic experience and prediction. By psychic experience, I mean that they want to be wowed by the information you have plucked from their mind—like their cousin's first name or the fact that their dad was a plumber. You can also do that by telling them something about themselves such as their favorite color or personality trait. If you can read palms, or know something about astrology, both of these can certainly wow someone looking for that psychic factor. You can also do a general tarot reading to reveal a question or issue currently present in the guest's life. The other thing they're looking for, prediction, is straightforward. They want to know how something is going to turn out.

If a guest wants the former, they usually will say things like, "what does the universe wish to tell me?" or "You're the psychic. You tell me!" They tend to be "mum's the word" in order not to tip you off. In most cases, you won't have time to give everything they desire, so I tend to give them a choice. Would you like a palm reading, a general reading with tarot, or is there something on your mind that you would like a specific prediction about? Guests can use up a lot of their allotted time making a decision here, so you will want to get them to make it quickly.

I really want to stress that you need to maintain control of the whole guest experience from the second they sit down until they stand up to leave. You are leading the dance, and you are going to walk them through the moves in a way that will hopefully give them a good experience within the time limit. It's like when you have a group of kids and you want to get them ice cream. You don't want to say, "What flavor do you want?" You are going to be there all day. You need to give them an easy choice, "Do you want vanilla or chocolate? Cake cone only." If the kids aren't really aware that you have jettisoned the other 29 flavors, they will happily give you an answer within your parameters and feel like they still had a choice. Reading for guests is exactly the same. Of course, if you are doing a house party and have 20 minutes or more per guest, you may not need this technique, but for large venues this works quite nicely.

Do the Shuffle

I don't ask my guests to shuffle because about ninety-five percent of the time they will say, "I'm a terrible shuffler!" They will give a painful attempt at shuffling that makes them feel embarrassed, or they will bend my cards in ways that physically pain me. I don't want my guest to be stressed out about shuffling. Instead, I'll shuffle and then have them tell me to stop when it feels done. Sometimes I cut the cards into three piles and ask them to pick the one from which I will read. I might fan out all the cards from the chosen pile or let my guests choose from the top. Whichever way I decide depends on time and event. I've tried every which way regarding shuffling and choosing cards, and they all produce accurate readings. This is one of the things I love about tarot: the loosey-goosey factor.

Reading Choreography

To help you craft each reading instance it might help to choreograph your reading sessions for a five-, ten-, fifteen-, twenty-, and thirty-minute delivery. *The thing to keep in mind is that a guest will ask the same kinds of questions regardless of how much time they have.* You will have to learn how to give answers to, "Will I get this job?" in five, ten, fifteen, and twenty minutes. You can talk about the outcome whether you have five or twenty minutes but with more time you can flesh out the answer by providing more details.

From beginning to end create a "screenplay" of what is going to happen at each step and for how long. This is a tall order! Within a short time frame, you are being tasked with entertaining them, amazing them and giving them relevant information. It's a lot to nail down, and you are processing a large amount in quick succession to make sure you are doing it well. This is why your beginning beta parties for friends and family are so important. These beta sessions give you the time you need to nail your choreography perfectly.

While you might have your session choreographed to the second, your guests should feel an organic, rather than formulaic, process. Like watching a magician, they will only see the rabbit being pulled from the hat, but you are toggling levers and pressing buttons behind the curtain. It's a delicate balancing act that will get easier the more you practice.

Guests may not understand the need for you to keep time, and if they are not the ones paying, they *really* don't care about staying on time. They might have one more question or use you as a therapist–talking the whole time then want a reading in the last minute. They may change their mind on what they want. They might call their friends over to listen in. They might spill their drink on the table. They might even clam up entirely. You have the challenge of "herding cats" into strict blocks of time. You can only do this by maintaining control of the entire process. You have to learn how to redirect a guest who is on a tangent and you have to learn how to end a reading with a guest who wants to stay. All of these will require you to be charming, have a good sense of humor, and quick on your feet.

Quick or Thorough

Whether you've been hired to read for five minutes or a full thirty, each guest requires a unique set of tools for the challenges they present. *You can be quick, or you can be thorough but rarely both.* I find that readings have a way of going deep or going wide and while a guest would like both, you most likely don't have the time.

Five Minutes: Five-minute readings are challenging with general readings. There is just so much information and so many ways the cards can go, but there is not a lot of time to explain it all. I will ask a guest for a question and if they don't have one (usually they don't) I will offer them a list of focus areas such as: relationship, career, finances, home, children, and so on and ask them to choose one area. Once I know what we are looking for, I will shuffle and read the cards from the top. I will read up to five cards in a line without any specific positional meanings. Let tarot do the work here, it will speak to you and to them even under these conditions.

Longer Readings: For ten-minute readings and up, I use an all-purpose spread that works well. I have guests pull three cards each on the following areas: love, money, career, health, and spirit. This gives me a nice bit of information and guests are usually satisfied. I included a sample of this general reading in the appendix. For my twenty- to thirty-minute sessions, I may often turn to Lenormand and do a quickie Grand Tableau for them or even a Celtic Cross spread with tarot.

Reading Sequence

Here is a format that might help you build your reading choreography. You can make these as long or as succinct as you need.

Introduction Sequence: This is where they sit down, settle their drink and introductions are made. Always ask for their name and use it repeatedly through the session. Using their name and giving yours creates a quick sense of familiarity and builds rapport. You need rapport for good readings. Always seek to build that as fast as possible. Sometimes, I will compliment a guest. It is always honest though, if I legitimately like their shirt, ring, or hair I make sure to tell them.

Question Sequence: Here you ask whether they have a question and determine how you want to give them their reading. (You can lose a lot of precious time here, so if they do not immediately have something in mind, move to a general reading.) You can also just give them two options to choose from.

Shuffle Sequence: Decide how you want to shuffle, hold, fan, or display your cards. Of course, this will change depending on how much time you have. When I have more time, I like to make this intricate.

Reading Sequence: This is when you conduct the actual reading wherein you have timed the spread and your explanation. Remember, while each guest gets ten minutes, each reading is actually closer to seven once you add up for all these other factors. *Make sure to nail your timing.*

Closing Sequence: This is when you verbally state that your time with them is almost done, I do this between three to five minutes before the actual end (depending on total length of the session). I may have them pick a closing card or oracle card. *It's important to lead them towards the end before it is the actual end.* This makes transition easier.

Goodbye Sequence: I tend to give a minute or two here to thank them, send them their recording (for longer readings), hand them my card, answer any quick questions (such as, can you come to my house, too?) and allow them to grab their drink and leave my table.

For readings that are fifteen minutes and above and in a reasonably quiet place (usually a house party), I will record the session and send it to each person. I either use an online service, or just record them with the voice memo app on my phone. I send the recording right away at the end as part of my closing sequence or the next day. Usually, I will have the host collect email addresses so I have permission to contact them. The next day I will send them a follow-up thank you email with a giveaway document (something I think they may be interested in like "how to do a house clearing"). I might also include a code for a discounted full session with me at a later date.

Tarot Don't Care

Tarot is going to say what it needs to say. Tarot doesn't care about venue, event, mood, or atmosphere. Tarot's role is to impart information, give predictions and provide insight. That is what it's made to do. As you know, tarot does not mince words. Our work as party readers is not just to translate what tarot is telling us, but to do it in ways that will honor the entertainment agreement we have made with the host.

At house parties, guests usually want a deeper experience in session. For events like a Bachelorette party or Bridal Shower, though, we want to keep things light. It takes a certain finesse to impart the message of tarot (who loves being the kid to shout the emperor has no clothes) without ruining anyone's day. You would think that at a party, people wouldn't ask certain questions, but I've had some real doozies such as, "Is my husband cheating on me?" or "I have cancer. When will I die?" Yikes! Do you really want to talk about this at Aunt Gretchen's 60th birthday soiree? When this happens, I simply say no. I'm direct. I tell them that the question is too deep for such an atmosphere while handing them a card and telling them to make an appointment.

Another modification is to use a gentler deck where the so-called "bad" cards are not as obvious or dramatic. As you probably know, the moment someone pulls the death card they freak out, even when we tell them that it doesn't mean literal death in most occasions. Keep in mind that guests tend to weigh negative cards more heavily than positive ones. We as humans have cognitive biases, and the negativity bias is a huge one. Most guests, even when given ten wonderfully positive cards, will zero in immediately on Death and the Devil. They will ask about it; wanting clarification even when it's not a major factor in context with the entire reading. When you use a gentler deck where the imagery is not so obvious, you can steer the message to be heard while avoiding knee-jerk reactions.

A few years ago, I was reading at a high-end event. There were other party service professionals like me, providing different forms of entertainment. My little corner of the party was quiet, and I had more than the usual time to spend with each guest. I was approached by a couple, and the woman sat down asking for a reading about her health. Some readers refuse to read for health questions. I think every reader needs to determine for themselves what they are comfortable reading. As for myself at events, I usually read for more wellness than an actual targeted health reading. I'm looking at lifestyle factors that affect health, but I am not trying to check on whether your colitis is having a good year.

As I laid the woman's cards out, I could see that she had just lived through something that was against the odds. While I had spread out all the cards for her reading, I was only looking at the first few as I was talking. Out of the corner of my eye, I felt her partner growing uncomfortable, so I looked up at what he was staring at. Right there, in the final outcome, was Death. And by Death I do not mean "transition state." It looked clear to me that this woman was in remission and the time she had now would be short.

Right then, the DJ made an announcement, and the host gave a little speech. While my guests were looking away, I switched the Death card with the Hanged Man. When they turned back to finish the reading the partner looked confused. Clearly there was a different card than what he saw before.

Because we were at a party, I made the decision to give her a lighter version of what the cards indicated. I told her that her health was something she needed to continue to focus on proactively, but in the meanwhile live life to the fullest. I told the truth as close as I could without ruining the party for them.

The tarot was extraordinarily clear about what it wanted to tell her. My mistake was assuming she wanted a general light-hearted health reading (while what she actually wanted to know was whether the cancer was going to stay away). This is another danger of general readings because I have noticed that general readings often lead tarot to bring forth the most salient thing it wants you to know—whether you are ready or not. *Like honey badgers, tarot just don't care!*

Because of tarot's tendency to overshare inappropriately, some readers make the decision to take out the "scary cards." Pulling out Death, the Tower, the Devil, 10 of Swords, and so on, helps ensure that the message is kept on the lighter side. Honestly, I go through phases about how I feel about this practice. Sometimes, I'm adamant, "How dare you break your deck!" and at others phases I've broken my deck when specifically asked by hosts to not give any "scary readings." *When I've taken out the heavy-hitters, I've noticed that tarot still finds a way to get the news across, but I can interpret as in the way I need to for the environment.*

Finally, you could also have a standing rule on certain types of questions you will not answer at a reading and add it to your contract. Some readers won't answer any questions related to health, divorce, death, or debt. Some readers will faithfully answer any question put to them. Again, there is no hard and fast rules here. Rather, you need to decide what you are comfortable doing and what works towards the best interests of the party. I recommend you say no if you think it's going to mean someone ends up crying in the bathroom.

Gallery Readings

Gallery readings are formats where you are reading for one person but a whole audience is listening in. You could have a small group of people, like a dinner party table of ten, up to hundreds with you on stage. Gallery readings are great fun, but I would consider them to be advanced-level party readings. This is the kind of reading where you need to be confident in your skills, have a bit of showmanship, and be able to manage any potential stage fright. The gallery reading set-up is where you are reading for an individual in front of an audience. What makes a gallery reading fun and unique is that you are able to play with other guests and get them to comment or laugh about the reading you are giving to their friend. Some parties may ask that you do a gallery style reading, and it's up to you to agree. Like I shared earlier, a house party wanted a gallery style reading "Real Housewives" style and I kiboshed it. For public events, however, where people tend to be well-mannered, it can go over quite well.

In most cases, I don't do more than a three-card spread for each person. I also ask for specific questions. I might start off with an intro about tarot, clairvoyance, and my background. I'll also lay down some ground rules such as "no dead people" or "no health readings" or "no lottery numbers."

While I'm roving around giving mini readings to individuals, I do not need a table to lay out cards. I discovered a little technique that has served me well. While standing, I will do an overhand shuffle with the cards facing up. At each break in the shuffle, I see a card. Each overhand shuffle shows me about three to four cards in the cuts. From there, I get my reading.

Gallery readings can be lucrative. This is why you see a lot of mediums doing gallery style readings. I'm a regular reader for a psychic gallery, and my friend (the host) has a deal with a local restaurant. He gets to use their back room for two hours, free of charge, as long as the crowd is eating and drinking above a certain amount. (They always do.) Each guest pays ten dollars, and the room holds sixty people. The room books out every time because ten bucks is a pretty low bar for entry. It's easy to do the math here: the room makes six hundred dollars for two hours. My friend keeps two hundred for the work he puts into marketing and coordinating, and I keep a cool four hundred for two hours of my time. I have no other venue that pays as handsomely as quickly as that! Not every guest will get a reading, but within two hours I can quickly read for about twenty people—enough where many get a reading but pretty much everyone is entertained. Treat these gallery readings as commercials for your skills. These guests will often book you for longer sessions or invite you to their own events.

At Ease, Reader

It's fair to assume that most of your party guests have never had a reading before or that they have a superstition about it. Tarot has long been shrouded in mystery and has an "other worldly" factor that may intimidate some people. Keep this in mind as you set the tone for your guests. Make them feel at ease by being friendly, open, and patient. Assume that they know nothing about tarot besides the most topical pop cultural references. Some guests are operating under old models about tarot being bad or even dangerous. Your attitude can change both of these biases, *so don't get defensive*. When you are confident and comfortable with your work, people will pick up on that. That alone can be enough of an opening to change their point of view.

Your role is to help guests feel comfortable. If they are nervous, address it. If they have questions about the process, encourage them to share it with you. It takes a lot of gumption for some people to even just sit at your table. Ease fears, relax anxieties, and always leave them better than you found them.

Party Guests

I can set my watch to the type of guests I typically get. Allow me to outline the usual suspects and how I deal with them so you can build an internal script for handling each one when they appear. These, of course, are outlining those pesky five percent. I figure you already know how to interact with the pleasant ninety-five percent who will come to your table.

First-Timers: You'll encounter a lot of tarot newbies when reading at public and corporate events. These guys are fun because they often don't have a lot of expectations and are open to your process. They might also be nervous, so work to put them at ease as soon as possible.

Read My Mind: It's a common belief that the way to test a "true psychic" is to see whether they can pluck information from your mind. They want to see whether you are a fake or not. They usually do this by refusing to say anything or by hiding a tell (like a wedding ring) to not tip you off. If you have a short reading, you have to push back because you don't really have time to play this game. Not to mention the fact that this approach is annoying. I'm clairvoyant, but my clairvoyance refuses to play when it feels like it has to "prove" itself. Usually, I just call out their game in a friendly way. "I get that you don't want to tell me anything, but with our limited time I really need a question to work with." Don't let them bully you into playing a script you are uncomfortable with. Maintain control by kindly calling out the behavior and offering an alternative.

Once I was working for a vintage clothing store during a Philly's First Friday event. These First Fridays are evenings where local businesses throw their doors open and provide snacks and entertainment to all who wander in. I loved working this gig every year because the hosts were excellent;

they would help wrangle the line and were respectful of my boundaries. But, because we were getting people right off the street, I would occasionally encounter some challenging people.

At this event I had a guy sit down at my table and say, "What can you tell me about my love life?" Now, when a person is intentionally trying to throw you off, it can be confusing because the cards will you show you something you might doubt because of the way the guest phrased their question. The tarot cards were talking about a marriage, but I was confused because he framed his question in a way that sounded like he was single. So, while the cards were clearly telling me one thing, my rational mind was trying to read something different.

I felt the reading was fighting me the whole time because I nuanced his question rather than reading what I was actually seeing in the cards. It was tough! So, I pushed ahead and told him what I thought. He answered, "Oh well, that is all interesting, since I'm married!" As soon as he said that, everything shifted into place. The fighting I was doing with the reading was gone; everything was clear. I said to him, "Why didn't you tell me that? Because that changes everything!" I proceeded to read for him again. As you can guess, I was accurate and on point. This guy was trying to test me, but what he ended up doing was confusing me. My intuitive mind was right, but my rational mind was fighting for control. With short readings, there isn't a lot of time to build rapport, so it's perfectly okay to ask questions until you are clear on what they are actually asking about.

For example, let's say you have seven minutes to give a reading. A guest sits down and says, "I want a love reading." You can respond by asking them to nail that down. "Do you mean your marriage had a rough patch, and you want to know how to get it on track? Are you single and wondering if anyone new is coming your way? Do you feel like you've been ghosted because you haven't heard from Tyler in three days?" When you can get them to nail down what they actually want, then you can spend your time on providing the answer and details rather than wasting time on figuring out from the cards what the question actually is.

Skeptics: Corporate events have the highest percentage of skeptics. They are not paying, they are just milling around at the party, so why not mess with the reader a little? I'm sorry to say this but the vast majority of these types are guys in suits with "superiority boners." Their only goal is in preening with their "obvious" intellectual and moral egotism. The way I handle them depends on how I'm feeling at the moment. Some days I feel riled up, and when I am, I will proceed to give them a reading that shuts them up. You know, the kind of reading where you dredge up the fact that the IRS is after them and their kid just failed math. They will sit there with their mouths hanging open. I have to admit, I'm bad, sometimes!

But more often, I will just flatter them and try to get a tip instead. I'll focus less on the reading and more on telling them something to make them feel good. However, the moment they are overtly disrespectful I will call out the behavior, and if it gets belligerent, I tell them to leave. Usually though, this stuff is subtle. The point is, don't let these fools intimidate you. They have small hands and big egos. They are truly not worth getting upset over.

Kids: When it comes to parties like a family function, you will get young kids wanting a reading. Kids love tarot, they immediately notice and are attracted to it. As a rule, I personally do not read at events for minors such as Bar Mitzvahs and Sweet Sixteen parties (though many readers do). That's just my personal preference. However, when I'm at a family function I won't turn kids away. I will though, use a softer deck, perhaps an animal-oriented oracle deck. I also keep the readings topical and child appropriate with questions like "how is school?" or "is my family going on a trip?" or "am I getting a puppy?". If you have a firm policy about reading for minors, make sure you have included that in your contract and that your host understands.

Non-stop Talkers: These guests can be frustrating because if you let them talk the entire time, they will later complain about how they didn't get a reading. Lady, I can't read and listen to you talk at the same time! You have to find a way to interrupt them so you can give them what they came for. It's okay to be perfectly transparent here, often we are socialized to not interrupt people, but in this case, you need to. You can say something like, "What you are saying is so poignant, and I would love to listen to your story, but I only have x amount of time and I want to give you the reading you sat down for."

Won't Leavers: These are similar (and often the same as) your Non-stop Talkers. The Won't Leavers don't care that there is a line of fifty people behind them; they want a reading and they want to sit and spill their tales of woe onto you. Both the Non-stop Talkers and Won't Leavers are attempting to control YOUR process. With the Won't Leavers, I tell them that their turn is up. If they continue to try to manipulate the situation I simply stand up and raise my arm, whole hand open and pointing towards the exit. If you have a tight reading choreography you should be able to handle these guys easily but if you are a gentle soul with less than ironclad boundaries, they can sense that and take advantage. Be tough yet polite.

Couples: It's quite common to have a couple (romantic partners, best friends, or mother and daughter) wish to have a reading together. Once, I was working at the grand opening of a high-end furniture company in downtown Philadelphia. I had a couple sit down and say they wanted a reading together. I pulled a mini reading for each of them concerning what they each were bringing to the table. As I was doing so, the couple started telling me that they met on a dating app two days prior and were on a whirlwind weekend-long date. I could tell from the cards that, while the guy was totally into the girl, she was seeing the weekend as more of a fling and not really interested in a long-term kind of thing. What a sticky situation!

It took a lot of politicking to get through that reading. The woman and I exchanged glances. She knew that I knew the real deal, but the poor guy was sweetly basking in what he felt was his newfound love! I decided to handle the reading by talking about their personality types when it comes to relationships and their communication styles. He came up as a King of Cups and she was the Queen of Swords. (I know, right?!) So I emphasized his need for affection and her desire to talk things out.

With couple's readings it's very easy, laughably easy, for all the dirt to come back out from under the rug. Handle readings like this with great care. Avoid touching the messy topics but do try to give them advice or clarity. If you decide that this is a can of worms you don't want to open, then it's totally fair to enforce a blanket "no couples" rule.

Interjectors: Some guests will feel the need to interject with a comment (to agree, disagree, expand upon, etc.) with every single card or sentence you utter. For me, this kind of guest is hard to navigate because being constantly interrupted absolutely messes with my train of thought and my ability to perceive intuitive messages. I make sure to stop them or tell them something like, "Please keep your comments and questions until the very end of session."

There's Always One: In every single event, there is always "that one person" who comes in shut down, defensive or even downright hostile. First off: *it's not you*. This person could be the odd one out at the party or are having a bad day. Maybe the cheese plate was empty by the time they got to it. Whatever the case, this person is not having it, and they will project all of that unsavory energy right onto you. You, being the sensitive reader that you are, may be more affected by these types than the average person. You need to find a way to ground their energy in a way that does not hamper your work. Count on having one of these guests and know that there isn't anything you did to make it so.

It's easy to let them get under your skin, but that will affect the readings to follow, and as you know, if you are not confident, those readings will suffer. I make it a game, so when the one shows up, I check it off my internal list knowing that it I can continue with party readings as scheduled. Honestly, they are a perverse kind of good luck, like rain on a wedding. If I don't get one, I now feel oddly incomplete. I have some energetic tricks you can use when dealing with these kinds of people, I include them in chapter five.

Travel Kit

Your life will become so much easier as a party reader if you have a standard Go Bag or Travel Kit for your gigs. Having these things packed and ready to go creates a calm and smooth process to planning your party reading. Here is what I have in my Go Bag:

Travel Bag: I have a large canvas bag on wheels that is one of the most amazing things I own. It holds a lot, is light to carry, and I can wheel it around.

Tarot Deck: Keep one just for parties that stays in the bag. I recommend one that is worn in, so you won't get blisters from shuffling. It's a good idea to make this deck one that won't break your heart if it gets messed up—the kind of deck that you can easily replace should a beer or a Cosmo spill on it if the cards get bent by the guests. Your party tarot deck needs to be a workhorse. Leave your Kickstarted, out-of-print lovelies at home. The deck should be topical for a mass audience. If there is too much nudity or if the deck is too dark in content it will make some people uncomfortable. I use themed decks (like my *Zombie Tarot* for Halloween) if it feels appropriate. *Make sure that you count your cards before and after every event.* It's incredible how easily one or two can get lost.

Tablecloth: I already talked at length about tablecloths and table runners, so I will not belabor the point. Just add these to your Go Bag and make sure they are the wrinkle free kind of fabric.

Crystals: I like the ambiance of crystals. If they are small enough, they are easily transportable. I like to bring crystals that have properties that will help me in a reading. Black Onyx, Black Tourmaline, Lapis Lazuli, Amethyst, and Chalcedony are great for psychic protection, so I have a bag of these. Rose Quartz promotes compassion and empathy, so it's another useful stone to have on your table. Finally, I might wear jewelry that is attuned for me and my protection such as Smoky Quartz.

Candles: I'll bring a candle that has a lid on it and a lighter for appropriate situations. You may need a candle that comes with a lid because usually you'll have just blown out the wick and the wax will be wet as you are packing up and leaving. I try to blow them out about fifteen minutes before I'm finished so the wax hardens up a bit before I go. Keep in mind that some people are sensitive to scents. A lot of readers will bring the battery-operated candles where live flame is not allowed.

Business Cards/Promotional Items & Holders: I always bring my business cards, and I have a lovely dish to hold them in. I place this dish near the right-hand side of the guest.

Disclaimer: Make sure you have copies for everyone and a few more, just in case.

Party Favors: For smaller house events I offer party favors. Currently, I use those small "fortune telling" Swedish Fish that come in their own jacket. I slip my business card in the gift and bring one per guest.

Tip Jar: I have a pretty, hand-thrown pottery bowl that I will seed with a few bucks to be placed near the business cards (provided it's appropriate and I have permission to accept tips). Of course, this is US-based advice, the culture of tipping varies by country.

Clipboard: I have a travel-sized clipboard that I bring when people need to sign up in advance.

Journal/Notebook & Pens: These are always useful for jotting down notes, writing things down for guests and so on.

Travel First Aid Kit: I was a Girl Scout, what can I say?

Florida Water: I pack a bottle of Florida Water or one of my Space Clearing Mists to sprinkle around the area if I am able.

Throat Lozenges: These guys are indispensable for me and a real life saver to my voice.

Lip Balm: Again, all that talking gets my lips dry, so some minty lip balm is refreshing in the thick of sessions.

Wet Wipes and Hand Sanitizer: Don't let Jimmy's cold take you down next week!

Pain Killers: For that pesky last-minute headache or back pain, always nice to have on hand.

Dry Erase board and Markers: Have a small board on hand so you can tell guests where the line begins. These are super handy to have.

Card Swiper: At some events I'll take individual payments. If that is the case, then I bring a card swiper that attaches to my phone. Or, you can download an app that allows a direct payment without having to swipe a card.

Timer: A timer is essential for keeping you on track with your guests. You could also just use your phone but be mindful of battery usage when the screen is on for hours at a time. I tend to not allow my guests to see the timer because they will then demand readings to the very second. This is for my own use to make sure that I am hitting each mark when I need to, it is not for them to make sure I am giving them the appropriate amount of time.

Tissues: Tarot's profound ability to strike at the heart of the matter can be so surprising that people will sometimes cry. Having some tissues on hand is a kind gesture.

Things to Pack Day Of:

Device: I like to record longer sessions for guests, so if there is Wi-Fi, I will bring my Chromebook. It's small and unobtrusive. An iPad or Android tablet may be what works for you. (As obsolete as this will be in a year or two, bring whatever technology you need to do the job.)

Device Plugs: You might be able to plug your devices nearby.

Battery Bank: Fully charge your external battery so your phone doesn't run out of juice!

Printed Out Directions: I cannot tell you how many times my GPS failed or my phone died and what saved me was a good, old-fashioned print out. I can't say enough about having this analog failsafe.

Water: You can't assume the host will take care of this for you. If you are working late, you might want to pack a caffeinated beverage, too.

This list is by no means exhaustive. Consider this a starting place as you build what will work for you. I am sure you will find some things unnecessary and other things indispensable. Try to pack light and look for what is efficient and quickly accessible. I included it again in the appendix so you can quickly find it when you need it.

Repeat Business

One-and-done mentality is running rampant in business these days, but I think the best ways to build a business is to cultivate a relationship of trust. If we are careful and respectful of the gift of intimacy, we can develop a relationship that will last. We can only cultivate stable, long-term relationships by coming from a place of deep authenticity.

Your business is an organic being; it creates relationships as it ebbs and flows. Therefore, your marketing should work like an interlocking mechanism. Everything fits into everything else. Keep in mind that, dollar-for-dollar, it's cheaper to market to repeat guests than to new ones. Your diligence as a professional reader is to create sustainable relationships with people who will return to use your services. We encourage repeat business by engaging in thoughtful customer service. In fact, it is a bad sign if you only ever get new clients and the old ones do not return.

Because repeat business is so important, it is necessary to capture client information so you can communicate to them your various offerings. You can offer promotional items such as raffles and giveaways or collect phone numbers or email addresses for a chance at winning a free reading. If you have a newsletter, use it. People like the personal touch. You can even send a simple text or email to them, and it should be noted that both of these options are more direct than social media platforms.

While you are working at an event, you are auditioning for more work in the future. Every guest is a potential client, host, student or referral source for you to explore. Think about how you can keep these relationships long after the bottle of wine has been kicked.

5
Vibe Attracts Tribe
What's your frequency, reader?

Metaphysical Properties

If you are not a believer of metaphysical properties, known colloquially as *energy*, you can skip this section entirely. In fact, I know some great readers who are anti *woo-woo*. They don't smudge, they don't charge crystals during a full moon, and they say that they aren't affected by vibes. Fair enough.

But when it comes to "energy", everyone is different. What one person doesn't see or feel could be a sensitive person's emergency. My advice here comes from my own level of energetic needs and protections. Since these are highly individualistic, take what works but leave the rest. I merely share these with you to give you a sense of the framework I am working from. Perhaps they can help you, too.

I aim to keep this chapter light and focused on basic energy care. There are so many ways to navigate the vibes you encounter in a party reading situation that it really depends on your spiritual beliefs, on your sensitivity, and on your comfort level with these kinds of things. Honestly, a whole book could be written on this aspect alone!

Grounding and Centering

Grounding and Centering is an incredibly important healthy habit. It is so vital, that I include it in my private practice. And while it is, of course, important to ground and center yourself whenever performing work that brings you in contact with other people's energy, my focus here is about grounding and centering your client.

In one-to-one sessions, I ask each client to hold (not shuffle) the deck. With their eyes closed, I ask them to take a deep breath and to bring their attention to the present moment. Once I sense they are present-minded, I ask them to quietly introduce themselves to the deck. After that, I will take them through a very quick thirty-second guided meditation that I channel on the spot which is tailored to their question: for one client, I might have them stand at a crossroads while another watches a bottle wash up on shore. I find this process takes less than three minutes, and it makes for a powerful and receptive reading.

Since I do not have the luxury of grounding and centering with each guest at a party reading, I have to do it for the both of us. My personal grounding and centering practice begins before I even enter the building. This step is to create intention for my work. What is my role here? Who am I as a reader in this space? What do I need to remind myself of? How do I prepare for the work at hand?

Creating Intention: You might recognize this from the very beginning of this book. My Reader's Invocation is my pledge of intention. Saying this aloud or to yourself helps set the stage for the work you will be doing and helps to ground and center you at the same time.

Reader's Invocation

May the source of all that is Good, all that is Worthy, and all that is Meaningful speak to me through the cards.

May I be a kind interpreter, a helpful guide, and a noble facilitator of the story.

May I use my privileged position to increase perception, to foster compassion, and to perceive Spirit.

May I cast the lamp of insight high enough for clear vision, high enough to chase away the shadows of doubt, fear, and resistance.

May I withhold whatever is not helpful, what is unkind, and what is not ready.

May the weary feel the comfort of my care, the warmth of my affection, and the strength of my objective desire to witness their unfolding.

May I use tarot to guide and not to punish, to recommend and not to condemn.

May I be a servant to the Soul.

May I be a servant to the Message.

Most of all, may all who come feel safe.

Chakra Work: Another way I ground myself is to visualize a dynamic flow of chakra energy from my Crown Chakra to my Root Chakra. I visualize my Crown Chakra as a funnel of white light pulling higher vibrational energy into my body. This energy rushes down my body, activating each major Chakra along the way. I visualize it mingling with the indigo light of my Third Eye Chakra, and the light begins to change color, picking up each one along the way: blue from my Throat Chakra, green from my Heart Chakra, yellow from my Solar Plexus Charka, orange from my Sacral Chakra and finally, red from my Root Chakra. I then visualize this rainbow of energetic light sinking into the ground, firmly anchoring itself into the bedrock below me. I feel the dynamic tension of maintaining the circuit between earth and sky. This takes me about a minute. To the outsider, it just looks like I am sitting quietly.

Protect Yourself

Throughout the event you are connecting with people on a deeply personal level, and they are projecting all kinds of energy at you and on you. You'll deal with hostility, desperation, fear, loneliness, and depression as much as you'll see elation, joy, happiness, and peace. This is equivalent to standing within the blast zone of a nuclear detonation. Sure, I might look cute as can be in my party dress but energetically, I have a lead suit on.

Some readers visualize an orb of light surrounding their bodies or ask for the protection of a Spirit Guide or Angel. Again, this is all about your personal belief system–*you do you!* As for me, I bring the stones that I mentioned earlier as major protection devices. I also wear jewelry charged with protecting me while I work. I tend to enact further protections if I feel I need them, but while I am reading in public venues, I tend to keep it more reactive (handling energetic problems as they arise) rather than proactive (building an astral temple of protection through smudging, chanting, and so on).

With party readings it's usually impossible to do energy work in between each guest. Whenever I have a moment of quiet, though—usually as a guest is walking away from my table—I visualize cords running between them and me and a large pair of golden scissors in my hands. With a cutting motion, I cut the connection. If I am unable to do this with each person, I visualize a bunch of cords running from me off in different connections, and I cut them all in a bundle.

I believe I mentioned this before but it really needs to be repeated in this section, too. If I feel a sudden fatigue while reading for someone, this is a sign that I may be reading for an energy vampire. Energy Vampires are people who are able (usually unknowingly) to drain other people. Whether the energy drain is subtle or overt, the effect is very real. When I suspect that I might be reading for one, I make sure I don't look them in them in the eye. I look them between the eyes or at their forehead. This is an old trick for making sure you are not allowing yourself to be vulnerable to bad actors. It will still seem to them that you are looking them in the eye while you are not giving them an "in."

Touch the Deck: For years I wouldn't allow anyone to touch my deck. Then, I realized that I was actually hindering an important way to gather information. I've found that after someone touches my deck, I get impressions regarding their state of mind as well as images about what they are concerned about. Since people are touching my deck, though, it means that my deck can pick up energy that I will have to clear—which I will discuss in the next section.

Clear the Air

In my home office, I have the place "feng shui'ed to the hilt." Most people, even people who wouldn't consider themselves energetically perceptive, always compliment how nice my office *feels*. As a party reader, however, I have to take what I get. Have you ever walked into a building or room and instantly felt that there was something off? Locations hold energy, some good and some bad. Some places hold trauma from the events that have happened there, and they will affect how your cards will read for you.

There could also be spirits who will take an active interest in what you are doing and might attempt to use the reading to communicate. Ouija is not the only way to contact otherworldly bodies. I've used tarot for mediumship and house clearing, too. For all of these reasons and more, clearing the space around your table is highly recommended. My quick practice for clearing space is to visualize that I'm pushing my aura away from my body. As I do so, it gets larger, gaining mass until it fills the entire room. As it does so, it pushes out anything negative, destructive, or harmful. Once I've pushed everything out, I retract my aura back to settle around my body.

If I can get away with it, I will smudge the area with sage or sprinkle it with Florida Water. Most of the things I offer here can be done quickly. You should be able to ground and center, clear and protect within your fifteen-minute set-up time.

Deck Cleaning: My deck and I are partners, and I have to care for its energy as much as it looks out for mine. I'll notice that my deck needs extra love whenever it seems that the readings are turning particularly negative. Here is something I've been doing since I first started reading tarot: I'll tip my deck as if pouring a pitcher of water and visualize the dirty energy flowing out of the deck as dirty water out onto the ground. I then visualize clean water flowing from my Crown Chakra, down my shoulder, my arm and finally running through hand to the deck. Most people don't notice that I am doing this, and I can do it quickly.

Another one of my favorite cleaning practices is to reorder my deck from Fool to King of Pentacles. I might do this at the end of the night while I'm counting my deck to ensure I have all of my cards. If I feel I need to do more, I might smudge it with sage or lay my huge smoky quartz on the cards. Smoky Quartz is known for its clearing and grounding properties. I don't tend to do more than this, energy wise, but I do, listen to my deck and respect it when my deck is telling me it's done for the night.

Every deck has its own personality. I have some decks that are absolute princesses; they only want to be used in certain ways and will begin throwing off a reading if they feel disrespected. Other decks are workhorses; they'll keep reading and reading and have minimal maintenance needs. I never know how a deck is until I begin working with it, but it usually has nothing to do with how they look. If it feels like my deck is "tired"—you might be able to tell if the readings seem overly negative, or just shooting wrong, like you have to fight for the reading—I'll put it aside and read with another deck for a while. I treat them as good friends. I respect them, and when I do they speak to me loud and clear.

Clearing Personal Energy: Salt has long been believed to be a great purifier. The ancients noticed that salt halted corruption in food, allowing them to preserve it. It also has spiritual significance in that it will clear out negative energy from items as well. I use salt for personal use as well as house clearing uses, it's such an egalitarian (yet powerful) tool to have. I use salt to clear my energy after events when I'm in the shower. Some people prefer a certain kind of salt, but honestly, I think any will do. I have begun making my own salt scrubs by mixing salt with an oil of my choice. After I'm done cleaning my body, I finish by visualizing that I'm sloughing away any dark energy and replacing it with clean, protective energy. I recommend clearing from the top down but never the opposite. Allow the salt and oil mix to go down the drain along with any nasty energetic fingerprints.

I also use tuning forks in my private practice. I have forks that are tuned to specific Chakras as well as general "clearing" tuning forks. You can use these guys to both clear a room's vibration as well as clearing your own body. Additionally, in my office practice, I use tuning forks to clear energetic imbalances, so I will use them on myself if needed. Honestly, there are just a few of the things I do that work, but there are hundreds of different ways to handle energy clearing.

If I'm feeling really off, then I know I might be dealing with something "above my pay grade." There are many wonderful practitioners of the energetic arts that specialize in protection. If you get a sense that something you are doing isn't working, then I highly recommend you locate someone who can assist you in this process. At this point in my spiritual work, I keep things pretty simple, but I do hire people as needed when it's something I feel I can't handle on my own.

Conclusion

Can I talk seriously for a minute? I know—total party buzz-kill—but I want to finish by sharing with you a few things that are super important. These things will make the difference between a successful party reader, and a struggling one. I want you to triumph. I want to hear about how people said your readings were "freaking them out" and that they are "massively weird." These are compliments, by the way! I've given you my playbook for success, and I want you to use it for all its worth. I held nothing back. But knowledge is actually the smallest part of the equation.

A prosperous tarot business requires having two passions: reading tarot, and small business ownership. If you love tarot and only tolerate the business side, then this isn't going to work. You cannot fake this. You might find that Resistance and Self-Sabotage are the demons you must tackle. All the coaching and business books in the world will not work if you let those nasty imps within run amok with your efforts.

In fact, how you deal with inner-conflict in general is a key indicator for success. Can you get out of your own way by hacking your resistance, by moving past it when it shows up, by knocking on the door of that party even when your hands are shaking? Because this is what it means to be a professional tarot reader. The tool you need for this is discipline. You cannot wait to feel motivated to do the things that are hard or boring. You have to do them anyway. You cannot wait to feel confident to do the work, because confidence is the reward for having done the work already. *Confidence is a byproduct of success.* So, if you are waiting for Confidence and Motivation to show up before you begin, you are going to be waiting for a long time.

While writing this book I was certainly tackled by Resistance and Self-Sabotage. This book sat half-written for a year-and-a-half because I couldn't "pull it together in my head." Whatever that means. If you find yourself unable to understand or see something that you normally can, that's a sneaky weapon that Resistance deploys to stop you.

When I finally sat my butt down to finish this book, old Self-Sabotage showed up. She was mean and nasty with sentences like, "Who are YOU to write this book?" and "Your grammar sucks, you're not a REAL writer. Leave it to the pros." and "No one cares about a self-published book, only losers self-publish." I have to be honest, Self-Sabotage got to me. She really did. So, I reached out to friends to do a gut check. Are these things true? "Hell, no!" they said. I might have moped for a day but then I told Resistance and Self-Sabotage to kiss my butt, and I got right back to work.

But they are right to a point. There are better writers, better pro readers, and better party readers. My point is that there will always be someone who is better than you at something. But keep showing up. Do the work, resist these nasty inner-demons, and knock on that party's door.

I write this conclusion to you, dear reader, a few hours from a bachelorette party I'm working. There is a snow storm coming, so my client and her guests are holed up in an Airbnb to make memories of a lifetime. I will be part of that. I'm going to show up in a party dress with snow boots, ready to entertain them, to wow them, and perhaps in all of that, to help them, too.

This work is exciting. I get to meet lawyers, fire-walkers, fashion designers, the incredibly wealthy, the working class, the happy and the lost, the in-love and the broken. I get to meet life. Messy, questing, reaching life in all of its forms. What a fantastic profession to have!

Postscript:

My bachelorette party was a success. So successful, they left a review for me:

> 1. *Jenna was amazing! We had her come to the house as our day activity for my sister's Bachelorette and she was wonderful! Everyone really enjoyed and I would highly recommend her for a bachelorette. She was very easy to book with + provided some options [private readings or teaching tarot]. She was great at teaching tarot - we got to learn a lot, get some readings, etc. and it was fun to do it all together.*

I want this for you, too.
So, in closing, here is a blessing from me to you…

May your readings shine.
May your hosts book you, always.
May the guests be astounded with your work.
May you create engaging soul-work.
May this sustain you and lift you, invigorate and heal you.
May you be the conduit of the great, grand Mysterious Benevolence.
May you reveal what needs to be known, and may you safeguard what needs to remain unknown.
May you know success.

Time to Party!

Appendix I
Sample Proposal Letter

Queen of Wands Tarot
Engaging and Entertaining tarot for parties, events and festivals

"I booked Jenna for an event in my vintage shop for a First Friday. She was very accommodating, funny and pleasant to deal with. When we first met in person, I had an overwhelming urge to hug her. She is so warm and friendly.

She was fantastic in the shop, everyone who participated in the event raved about her. My personal reading from her was scarily accurate. If you are looking for a great tarot reading experience, look no further."

-- Betsy, Scout Salvage
and Vintage, Philadelphia, PA

Thank you very much for the opportunity to submit a proposal to your event! Queen of Wands Tarot has over twenty-five years' experience in reading tarot for events and large venues.

Queen of Wands Tarot is committed to creating a fun, unique and eerily accurate experience that will add that special *wow* factor. Your guests will be talking about your event and the reading they had there long after the event is done.

Queen of Wands Tarot proposes the following for your event:

4/1/2016 3PM to 6PM

Quote for the event: $360.00

Quote Includes:

- Reader table and two chairs if needed
- Professional and accurate readings that fit the theme and scope of the event
- Ongoing consultation as needed
- Travel and parking fees
- Set-up time of 15 minutes

Please review my website at www.queenofwandstarot.net for more information and testimonials. I hope you will consider me for your entertainment needs and I'm available at (phone number) or at (email) to discuss further.

Kind Regards,
Jenna Matlin

Appendix II
Sample Contract

Client Service Agreement

This Service agreement is entered into and effective as of this DATE, by and between John Doe ("Guest"), and Queen of Wands Tarot ("Company"), having an address of BUSINESS ADDRESS . The event location is HOST ADDRESS.

In consideration of Guest retaining Company to perform tarot readings, it's agreed as follows:

1. SCOPE OF SERVICES
Guest hereby retains Company to provide Tarot Reading services by purchasing Event Format Tarot readings service.

(a) The Event Format Tarot Readings Service includes the following services:

    (i) Travel to and from the event & set-up (15 minutes)

(ii) Decoration and costuming as directed by needs of the event

(iii) Furniture and other items as needed to conduct said service for event

(iv) Unlimited tarot/palm/Lenormand readings during agreed time of the event

(v) Promotion of event if needed

(vi) Breaks for the reader of five minutes every two hours

(b) Additional services, beyond those described above, will require additional fees to be discussed and agreed upon by the parties.

2. GUEST DUTIES

(a) Compensation: In consideration for the services provided by Company to Guest as set forth in paragraph 1 above, **Guest agrees to pay Company a project fee of PRICE ($XXX).** Company's obligation to render services hereunder is conditioned upon Guest's payment of said fee on a timely basis. **DEPOSIT AMOUNT ($XX) is due as deposit of the project.** <u>The balance of AMOUNT ($XX) is due upon project completion.</u> This does not include additional reimbursement for parking, (if needed) which can be handled at the time of the event.

(b) Tools to be provided by Guest: Guest agrees to provide all tools, information and documentation that may be required by Company to effectively perform said responsibilities in connection with the performance of services.

(c) Expenses: Guest agrees to reimburse Company for expenses incurred by Company solely on Guest's behalf, such as travel expenses, and the like; provided, however, that any single expense or related group of expenses must first be approved by Guest in writing, otherwise, Guest will have no obligation to pay such expense.

(d) Additional Guest duties: Guest is expected to provide water and access to bathrooms, reasonably safe working conditions, and a space adequate to provide tarot readings. Adequate directions to the location of the event and accurate contact information both prior to and during the event.

3. TERM

This engagement shall commence on **DATE from TIME until TIME** and shall continue through completion of the project or cancellation by either party in accordance with paragraph 4. Options for extension of time day of are negotiable at the time of the event.

4. CANCELLATION

Guest may cancel this agreement for any reason by providing a **minimum of 7 days** written notice to Company. Should Guest cancel the service within 7 days, Company will retain all submitted deposits. In the event that Company cancels this agreement, Company will provide a refund of any deposits.

5. NO GUARANTEES

Company cannot guarantee the outcome of Tarot reading services and Company's comments about the outcome are expressions of opinion only. Company makes no guarantees other than that the services described in Paragraph 1(a) shall be provided to Guest in accordance with the terms of this agreement. Guest acknowledges that Company cannot guarantee any results for foretelling the future or any information obtained through tarot as such outcomes are based on subjective factors that cannot be controlled by Company.

6. CONFIDENTIALITY

(a) Guest Information: any and all Guest information and data of a confidential nature shall be treated by Company in the strictest confidence and not disclosed to third parties or used by Company for any purpose other than for providing Guest with the services specified hereunder without Guest's express written consent. (b) Session information: all information obtained in a tarot session will also be held in strict confidence and not disclosed by third parties or used by Company for any purpose other than providing a Tarot session during the service agreement

(c) Non-disparagement: member shall, during and after the participation in and use of the Company's services, refrain from making any statements or comments of a defamatory or disparaging nature to any third-party regarding Company, or any of Company's officers, directors, employees, personnel, agents, policies, services or products, other than to comply with law.

7. INDEPENDENT CONTRACTOR
(a) Independent Contractor Relationship: Company shall retain sole and absolute discretion in the manner and means of carrying out the activities and responsibilities under this agreement. Guest retains the right to inspect, stop or alter the work of Company to assure its conformity with this agreement and Guest needs. Company and Guest agree to conform to any and all IRS tests necessary to establish and demonstrate the independent contractor relationship between Guest and Company. (b) Taxes & Benefits: Company will be responsible for filing its

own tax returns and to pay taxes in accordance with all provisions of applicable Federal and State law. Guest shall not be responsible for withholding taxes with respect to Company's compensation.

8. WARRANTIES

(a) Company's Warranties: Company represents, warrants and covenants that Company has full authority to enter into this agreement and that all of the services, whether performed by Company or any of its subcontractors, will be rendered using sound, professional practices and in a competent and professional manner by knowledgeable and qualified personnel. (b) Guest's Warranties: Guest represents, warrants and covenants that Guest has full authority to enter into this agreement and has or will obtain, during all times relevant hereunder, all of the necessary consents, rights, licenses, clearances, releases or other permissions to lawfully consummate the transactions and lawfully discharge, in all material respects, each and every of Guest's obligations or duties set forth hereunder, whether performance is due now or hereafter during the Term. (c) Except for the express warranties provided throughout this agreement, neither party makes any other warranties, express nor implied.

9. LIMITATION OF LIABILITY

In no event shall either party have any ability to the other party for any loss profits, loss of use, business interruption, costs of procurement of substitute services, or for any indirect, special, multiple, exemplary, punitive, or consequential damages however caused and, whether in contract, tort, or under any other theory of liability, whether or not the party has been advised of the possibility of such damage.

10. GOVERNING LAW; venue; mediation

This agreement shall be construed in accordance with, and governed by, the laws of the State of Pennsylvania as applied to contracts that are executed and performed entirely in Pennsylvania. The exclusive venue for any court proceeding based on or arising out of this agreement shall be Montgomery County, Pennsylvania. The parties agree to attempt to resolve any dispute, claim or controversy arising out of or relating to this agreement by mediation, which shall be conducted under the then current mediation procedures of The CPR Institute for Conflict Prevention & Resolution or any other procedure upon which the parties may agree. The parties further agree that their respective good faith participation in mediation is a condition precedent to pursuing any other available legal or equitable remedy, including litigation, arbitration or other dispute resolution procedures.

11. SEVERABILITY

If any term, provision, covenant or condition of this agreement is held by an arbitrator or court of competent jurisdiction to be invalid, void or unenforceable, the rest of the agreement shall remain in full force and effect and shall in no way be affected, impaired or invalidated.

12. SIGNATURES

In WITNESS WHEREOF, the parties to this agreement have duly executed it on the day and year first above written.

Company Name:

Signature:

Date:

Client Name:

Signature:

Date:

Appendix III
Sample Host Letter

Thank you for hiring Queen of Wands Tarot!

I am looking forward to reading for you and your guests! With a little preparation and some guidelines, we can ensure that everyone will have a great time. As always, if you have any questions please contact me at any time.

Please read over each section carefully. I will also be contacting you a few days prior to your event to coordinate any last-minute questions or logistics.

Reading Space

Noise: It is easy for me to lose my voice if I have to speak at a loud volume over hours at a time. Tarot readings should, ideally, be conducted in a quiet space. If you are hosting a party at home, another room or private alcove will do the trick. **If the party is at a venue where space is limited, I will need a space as far from the noise (such as music, DJ, karaoke**

machine, toasting area, etc.) as possible. For large events, something special to mark off this space helps create that 'reader vibe' for your party.

Furniture: A tarot reading space requires a table and two chairs. The table should be at a comfortable height from the chairs (like a card table or desk) and large enough to spread cards on. If you cannot provide these items, please speak with me as I can bring furniture that can accommodate these needs.

Decoration: Usually, the host will decorate the tarot reading area in accordance to their party theme and needs. However, I usually bring a black, white, and silver tablecloth, table runner and items that match that hold my promotional materials. If you have something unique in mind, I might be able to accommodate you, just let me know.

Travel Logistics

Living in the North East we have two realities: parking, and traffic. In many cases, I'm flying in blind. As a local, you'll have more information regarding traffic issues and parking so please communicate any tricky directions or logistics. If I'm bringing furniture to your event, we will need to coordinate loading of my gear to your event from my car. Also, **if your home requires a special code to enter, or if you live in a complex, please communicate clearly how to reach your home.**

Dress

Usually, I am dressed in all black and typically casual, but nice. If you have a themed event and wish that I dress to match, this can be arranged. Please note, however, that I do not dress as a 'tarot reading gypsy'. Cultural appropriation of the Roma's traditional dress is not something I am comfortable with.

Safety

<u>**If, for any reason, I feel safety is a concern or issue, I reserve the right to immediately end the event and the host is still responsible for the full payment of the event.**</u> Since I do not know your guests, it's up to you, the host, to ensure that a fun and safe time is had by all. I will not deal with behavioral issues while trying to read. If you have a guest that you know tends to imbibe too much, have them get a reading towards the beginning of the evening. If you have a

'negative nelly' you know is coming, alert me ahead of time so I can adjust their sessions accordingly. Also, I don't mind light flirting, it makes the evening fun but I have a zero tolerance policy on sexual harassment. As the host, I expect you to immediately back me up and remove the offender.

Refreshments

Reading tarot is thirsty work! Please ensure that I have water or another nonalcoholic beverage on hand and made available to me for the duration of the event.

Reading Times

If possible, I would like 8-10 minutes per guest in order to conduct high quality tarot readings. Intimate offerings can also include guests who are able to be seen for longer amounts of time, roughly 20-25 minutes each. For large venues I can conduct ultra-quick 6 minute rapid fire readings.

For larger venues, all readings are on a first come, first serve basis and there should be accommodation for a line so that people can get readings in an orderly fashion. For smaller venues, a list is fine with times for each guest. The host is responsible for providing this.

Breaks

I require a **5 minute break every 2 hours**, this is included in the time you are booking with me. Please ensure that you are booking enough time for the amount of guests you would like a reading for. I'm not always available to extend my time at the time of the event.

It's the Host's responsibility to ensure that there is enough time booked in advance for the guests. It's not the reader's responsibility to stay longer than the contracted time to accommodate more people.

Preparing Your Guests

Common tarot questions cover the following topics: finances, love, work, health, family, spiritual matters, decisions, and either-or scenarios. If you have skeptics, please encourage them to have an open mind! A closed-off guest makes for a difficult reading! Also, **I'm not a medium**, so please let your guests know that I will not be answering questions about the other side.

In order to prepare your guests to have a successful tarot reading, I've created several blog posts for tarot newbies. Please feel free to share this among your guests:

How to Get the Most Out of Your Tarot Readings:
http://www.queenofwandstarot.net/queen-of-wands-blog/how-to-get-the-most-out-of-your-tarot-reading

What to Do After Your Tarot Reading:
http://www.queenofwandstarot.net/queen-of-wands-blog/what-to-do-after-your-tarot-reading

What Does Tarot Do Besides Tell Fortunes?
http://www.queenofwandstarot.net/queen-of-wands-blog/what-does-tarot-do-besides-tell-fortunes

WIFI

For home-based events and if the sessions per guest is longer than 10 minutes, I will be able to record and email the sessions. Please provide the WIFI password at the beginning of the session so I can make this happen for your guests.

Alcohol

Queen of Wands Tarot certainly enjoys a tasty beverage here and again, and has no issues with guests who are enjoying themselves in the party atmosphere. **However, there will be times I'm unable to read for a guest who has been drinking excessively.** As host, your active support in this matter to help those curious but intoxicated guests understand why a reading may not be in the cards for them. Your support when making these tough calls is mandatory.

Minors

I only read for minors 16 and above with parental consent, and 18 and above without it.

Performance Agreement

For more information regarding our event as well as information on payment, please refer to the performance agreement.

Payment

I accept payment in cash or credit card for the amount due at the time of the event. If you would like me to use your credit card there is a **3.5% surcharge**. I only accept checks from businesses. No private checks will be accepted.

Gratuity

Gratuities are gladly accepted!

Thank you again, for booking me and I look forward to reading for your event! Communication is king! If you have any questions or want to let me know about something regarding your event, please do not hesitate to email me at: jenna@queenofwandstarot.net or shoot me a text at (phone number).

Thank you for hosting me!
Jenna

Appendix IV
Sample Receipt

<u>SALES RECEIPT</u>

Queen of Wands Tarot
ADDRESS
PHONE NUMBER
EMAIL ADDRESS
DATE: xx/xx/xxxx

SOLD TO
Jane Doe
Sample address, Sample City, State ZIP, USA

5 Hours Tarot Reading services for an event held on DATE in the amount of $XXX.XX has been paid in full. There was a gratuity of $XX added for services rendered.

Jenna Matlin
DATE

Appendix V
General Disclaimer for Tarot Services

By participating in my tarot service, you acknowledge that I'm not a licensed psychologist or health care professional, and my services do not replace the care of psychologists or other healthcare professionals. Tarot sessions are in no way to be construed or substituted as psychological counseling or any other type of therapy or medical advice.

Tarot sessions are for entertainment purposes only. I will at all times exercise my best professional efforts, skills and care. However, I cannot guarantee the outcome of the session and/or recommendations made in a Tarot session and my comments about the outcome are expressions of opinion only. I cannot make any guarantees other than to deliver the tarot services purchased as described.

Signed:
Print:
Date:

Appendix VI
Party Pack List

Travel Bag
Tarot Deck
Tablecloth
Crystals
Candles
Business Cards/Promotional Items & Holders
Disclaimer
Party Favors
Tip Jar
Clipboard
Journal/Notebook & Pens
Travel First Aid Kit
Throat Lozenges
Lip Balm
Florida Water/Clearing Spray
Wet Wipes and Hand Sanitizer
Pain Killers
Dry Erase board and Markers
Card Swiper:
Timer
Tissues

Things to Pack Day Of:

Device
Device Plug
Battery Bank
Printed Out Directions
Water:

Appendix VII
General Party Reading Spread

This is my handy-dandy go-to general reading spread for parties.

First, I pull out all the Aces. I also pull out the High Priestess to use as a focus card. These are set to the left.

Then I fan the rest of the deck in front of them. I will ask the guest to pull 3 cards at a time, 3 for each ace. Eventually, every ace will have 3 cards piled on top of it. I will ask the guest to place the High Priestess on a pile at random. This is the pile that I will emphasize during our time together.

I reveal one area one at a time and do a basic three card spread for each area. Your guest will get a basic reading about work (wands), relationships (cups), problem areas (swords) and resources (pentacles). This spread is best for a ten-to fifteen-minute reading.

For ten minutes or less, you can pick two aces to focus on and for five-minute readings you can have them choose one area.

Since most party guests want something predictive, it's fun to give them a choice such as, "Do you want to know the future of three weeks, three months, or three years?" You can combine this question with the Aces above.

Example Reading:

Clara's Five-Minute Reading:

One Area: Ace of Cups (love) — Pull Three Cards

In this guest's love reading, she pulled: Seven of Swords, Seven of Cups, & The Magician. Let's also say that Clara wanted the reading to be within the three-month timeframe. Here is how I would interpret this reading within five minutes:

"Hi Clara! Very nice to meet you!

Since you chose love within the next three months, here is what the cards have to say to you.

There will be some information revealed or uncovered (either information you concealed or that of another) that will cause you to consider a choice.

This choice could either be between partners or what do with the partner you have. After you make your decision there is no going back as you are committed to your vision. After a period of confusion everything will be made exceedingly clear like someone switched on the light. You'll know exactly what to do and how to initiate your plan of action. The Magician after the sevens indicate that once you focus on who and what you want, there will be no stopping you.

Thank you so much for reading with me! I would love to do a longer reading with you! Here is my business card and have a great evening!"

After Party

The wine has all been drunk. Around you lies the detritus of half eaten cupcakes and the host is nowhere to be seen.

You made it!

Before you go, **I have a request and a gift.** First, I offer my gift. I offer you PDFs of all my samples here for your downloading pleasure. If you would like that, please hop on over to my website using this link:

https://www.queenofwandstarot.net/willparty.html

Please note: The page is password protected because I am only offering my samples to people who bought *Have Tarot Will Party*. The samples mean nothing if you don't have a strong knowledge base to use them with!

The password is: *celebration.*

You will get a copy of my contract, disclaimer, proposal letters, and things I have not offered in the book like my programmable party rate calculator spreadsheet (seriously a lifesaver!). But I don't want to give all of the surprises away–you'll have to mosey on over to find out! *It does require you to sign up for a list*. I promise I won't spam you, but you might want to know when my next book is coming out!

Now comes my request. **Reviews, as you can imagine, are incredibly important.** Reviews tell others whether the work is suited for their needs. I don't think I even buy hairbrushes anymore unless I've read the reviews!

Review me on Amazon for this book, then email me (jenna@queenofwandsatarot.net) with a screen shot of your review and **I will give you a free PDF copy of my Have Tarot Will Travel 2016 updated edition as a thank you!**

Acknowledgments

There are some truly amazing people in the tarot community. I feel completely blessed to have had the ongoing support of so many. These people in particular have hearts of gold, backbones of steel, and smarts like nobodies' business.

I am in constant standing ovation to you:

Melissa Cynova: Your fierce loyalty, your kind open-heartedness is a gift to treasure.
Ethony Dawn: You are one brilliant, magical woman! Thank you for all of your generous support.
Jaymi Elford: You are such a real human being in the best sense of the word. Thank you for being there for me in some of my darkest hours.
Christiana Gaudet: You make me laugh so hard! I love the wisdom you always bring to the table, a wisdom tempered with light heartedness. Your friendship is treasured.
Arwen Lynch Poe: You are good, good people. Your heart speaks volumes, whenever I see the word, Joy, I think of you. Thank you for being you.

Theresa Reed: We go way back now, don't we? Thank you for always being in my corner. You are one hell of a woman. You show others how it's done as you lead by example. Your example is impeccable and your gastronomy is on point!

Benebel Wen: Last (well this is an alphabetical list) but certainly not least. You are one brilliant woman. I am in constant awe of your abilities, courage, and good heartedness. You go above and beyond in ways that astound me. I feel so lucky to call you friend.

Thank you to my beta readers: **Lauren Lowe, Katie Gray, Tasha Lee, Lori Lytle, and Kathleen Gubitosi.** This book is as good as it is because you fleshed out ideas, asked relevant questions that pushed me to go deeper, and were relentless with details and continuity. I am so grateful for you!

Finally, my last and most important acknowledgment. To the person who is always waiting in the wings, the one who is an endless source of joy, the person who believes in me and what I do with a fierce passion: thank you, **Rix White**. You are an incredible gift to my life.

About the Author

Jenna Matlin, M.S., is the clairvoyant engine behind Queen of Wands Tarot: (www.queenofwandstarot.net) a full-time tarot practice in Philadelphia. Jenna reads for both local and international clients, teaches classes, and coaches small businesses. Jenna is also the author of *Have Tarot Will Travel*, a DIY tarot business book focusing on festival work for the tarot professional.

Jenna Matlin was awarded the Tarosophist of the Year Award for 2016 and has spoken at Reader's Studio, the NorthWest Tarot Conference, and Tarot Con in Dallas, Florida, and Keswick, UK.

You can reach out to Jenna at jenna@queenofwandstarot.net. You can follow Jenna on Instagram, Facebook and Medium under the name of jennamatlin.

Made in the USA
Lexington, KY
22 February 2019